THE GAME OF
BASEBALL

GIL HODGES

Manager of the Mets

Player with the Los Angeles Dodgers

THE GAME OF BASEBALL

by Gil Hodges

with Frank Slocum

CROWN PUBLISHERS INC., NEW YORK

ACKNOWLEDGMENTS

I am profoundly indebted to many persons who helped me with this book. I owe a special thanks to my good friend and counsel, Sidney S. Loberfeld, not only for having brought my manuscript to the attention of the publisher, but also for his advice and exhaustive effort in my behalf. The book was written in response to the prodding of this sincere man, dedicated to baseball as a sport and as a discipline. I wish also to acknowledge the assistance of Lee Hazen, Harold Weissman, Dennis Burke, Jack Grossman of Field Studios, and Dr. Morris Pincus of the New York City school system.

TO MY BELOVED AND DEDICATED WIFE, WHO HAS
BEEN MY INSPIRATION IN LIFE'S MANY TOUGH GAMES

CONTENTS

INTRODUCTION

Sometimes they're called managers, sometimes they're called coaches, but whatever they're called, the job is pretty much the same. When you take into consideration all the sandlot teams, the high school and college teams, as well as the professional teams in this country, there's no way to guess how many have tried their hand at the job. There's only one thing you can be sure of. In one way or another, they all did it differently.

There's still another group of managers. They're the ones who sit in the grandstand. They're the lucky ones, because they have the luxury of the second guess. That isn't meant as a rap. Some of them are very knowledgeable about the game. They're experts on the so-called "book," the one that tells you what should be done in a certain spot in a ball game. There have been managers at all levels who also have been experts on the "book." The only trouble is that there's no such thing as that book.

Let's settle one thing very quickly. What you're holding in your hand doesn't pretend to be that book, either. In thinking about possible titles for this book, it was suggested that it might be called "How to Be a Winning Manager." There were two things wrong with that, the way I figured. One, if that was to be the title, the author should be Red Schoendienst. He's won two pennants in the last two years, and I spent both those years in the second division. The other thing wrong was that a book with that title might be a little shorter than most books. "How to Be a Winning Manager" is very simple. Have the right players. Otherwise, forget it.

Ballplayers make managers. Sometimes, managers make ballplayers, but not too often. Usually, all a manager can do for a player is to give him a chance to play. When I came up to the Brooklyn Dodgers, the manager was Leo Durocher. I was a third baseman then. From there I went into the service, and when I came out, I was sent to the Dodgers' farm club at Newport News, Virginia. They already had a first baseman, a fellow named Kevin Connors. You might remember him for brief stays with the Dodgers, and later the Chicago Cubs. But it's more likely that you remember him from a lot of movies, and some television series like "The Rifleman," "Branded," and "Cowboy in Africa." By that time he was "Chuck" Connors.

Chuck may have become a "Cowboy in Africa," but when I first met him he was a first baseman in Newport News, and I was a catcher. It took some getting used to, but I finally got to the point where I liked catching. As it turned out, I shouldn't have bothered getting to like it, because I wasn't going to do that much of it.

As a protection for the guys who went into the service, baseball had a rule that you couldn't be optioned out, without waivers, once three years had passed since you went on a major-league

The Dodger sluggers (from left): Duke Snider, Gil Hodges, Jackie Robinson, Pee Wee Reese, Roy Campanella.

roster. My brief stay at third base in Brooklyn took place in 1943. The next two years I was in the Marine Corps. After my year at Newport News, the club had to make a decision on whether or not to keep me. They decided that I could stay. Stay, but not play.

In 1947, I had a great seat on the bench as the Dodgers won the National League pennant. Durocher had spent that season under suspension, and Burt Shotton was the manager. Bruce Edwards was the regular catcher, and did a fine job. As I look back now, I realize that it was Edwards I was watching. Actually, the guys who were going to influence my career the most were Jackie Robinson, Eddie Stanky, Roy Campanella, and Durocher. But I didn't know that then.

In 1948, Durocher was back. Stanky had been traded to the Braves over the winter, and Robinson had been moved to second base. The first baseman in spring training was Preston Ward, a rookie.

That spring we trained in the Dominican Republic, and I had no idea that there were so many things happening that would change my life. For one thing, there was Roy Campanella. Campy had spent the previous year with the Montreal club, and he already looked like an outstanding player when he joined the club. But our big boss, Branch Rickey, had plans for Campanella that I knew nothing about. To me, Campy was a catcher, and a good one. But Mr. Rickey had him down to do a little pioneer work as well as catching.

It doesn't seem possible now, but things were a lot different in those days. There were no Negro players in the American Association, and Mr. Rickey wanted to change that. His plans called for Campy to go to the Dodgers' farm club at Saint Paul, and break the color line in the American Association. I know now about Leo's reaction to that. He was interested in civil rights, but he was more interested in winning, and he knew that the best catcher around was Campanella. He wanted Campy in Brooklyn.

But, like I said, Mr. Rickey was the boss, and Campy went to Saint Paul. Leo didn't like it, but it didn't bother me too much. I was looking for a job, and I was smart enough to know that it would be easier to get that job without Campy. When the season started, Edwards had a sore arm, so I was doing the catching, and Bobby Bragan was the number two man. I was more than a little confused about what was going to happen to me.

I didn't pay much attention to the fact that Preston Ward had fallen off a little at the plate, after a good start. Then, just like that, everything changed for me. I'd like to tell you that Leo called me in, and spelled it all out for me. That he gave me a big pep talk, and filled me with desire. But it didn't happen that way. Not quite.

It was late May, and all the ballplayers just sensed that things were getting ready to happen. I didn't know it, but the first thing involved me. Leo walked up to me in the clubhouse one day and said, "Son, if I were you, I'd buy a first baseman's glove, and start working out around there." That was it. The whole speech. So I bought a first baseman's glove, and started working out.

Then came the news that Durocher had finally won, and Campanella was rejoining the club. That meant that somebody had to leave to make room for him. At that time, the Dodgers' manager in Fort Worth was a fellow named Lester Burge. Just that quickly, Burge was out in Fort Worth, and Bobby Bragan went down to replace him.

All this gets me back to what I was saying. Managers don't make ballplayers. Durocher didn't take one look at me and say, "That's my first baseman." What he did do was to give me a chance to get into the lineup, and I'll always be grateful for that. But Leo and I both know that there were other factors. Stanky being traded was one. Ward having a slump was another. The fact that the Dodgers were forced to keep me on the roster was another.

Now, I find that I have to reverse myself on something. When I say that a manager doesn't make players, I'm talking about a major-league manager. Minor-league managers do, college and high school coaches do, and sometimes even managers in the various kid programs do, too. A little later, we'll get around to how they do it, and even how they fail to do it, too.

There are other areas in the job of managing that we're going to cover, and that includes grandstand managing. People in the stands are a lot more than dollars and cents to baseball, especially to the players. Nobody knows that better than I do. If it were possible for me personally to thank every one of the fans of the old Brooklyn Dodgers, I'd like to do it.

The support that they gave me wasn't good. It wasn't even great. It was unbelievable. When I was going good, they cheered for me. But they'll cheer for anybody anyplace, if he's going good. (There are some exceptions to that, and I'll talk about them later.) But the Dodger fans cheered for me when I was going badly. That's how you tell real fans, by how they react when you're in a slump. Take my word for it, I gave the Dodger fans a lot of opportunities to get on me. But they didn't do it.

I guess this is as good a time as any to get around to the 1952 World Series. (One day a reporter asked me about that Series, and I gave him a blank look, and said, "1952? Gee, I don't remember anything special about that one." He got such a funny look on his face, I couldn't help breaking up.) For the benefit of any of you who might not know the highlights of my playing career, 1952 was the year that the Yankees beat the Dodgers in seven games, and yours truly went to bat twenty-one times without getting a base hit. Not one.

The thing that most people hear about that one is that a priest stood in a Brooklyn pulpit that Sunday and said: "It's too hot for a sermon. Just go home and say a prayer for Gil Hodges."

Well, I know that I'll never forget that, but I also won't forget the hundreds of people who sent me letters, telegrams, and post cards during that World Series. There wasn't a single nasty message. Everybody tried to say something nice. It had a tremendous effect on my morale, if not on my batting average. Remember that in 1952 the Dodgers had never won a World Series. A couple of base hits by me in the right spot might have changed all that.

The point is that all managers, including the grandstand kind, can help a ballplayer. Maybe it's a tip on something to do with the game; maybe it's a word of encouragement; maybe it's even a blast that wakes a player up. Whatever it is, it *can* help.

One grandstand manager that I'll never forget was a guy who used to sit in the Polo Grounds. He was loud, and the bleachers were too far away, so he usually bought a box seat, where he was sure of being heard.

Well, this one day, we were playing the Giants, and we were winning. The first time the Giants needed a pinch hitter, Leo Durocher (now the Giants' manager) looked into the bench. Before he could make a sign, here came that loud voice from the box seats. He was hollering, "Wilson, Leo. Wilson." He was talking about George Wilson, a good left-handed pinch hitter the Giants had. But Leo went for Bill Taylor.

A little later, there was another pinch-hitting situation, and here came the voice again. "Wilson, Leo. Wilson." Only, this time he was a little louder. Again, Durocher decided to ignore him, and sent up Dusty Rhodes.

Now, it was the eighth or ninth inning, and Leo's got to get another pinch hitter. Again, the loudest sound in the ball park is this guy hollering, "Wilson, Leo. Wilson." Durocher made his move, and George Wilson came up to hit. He struck out on three pitches, and the Polo Grounds was quiet as he walked back to the bench. All of a sudden, the quiet was broken by a familiar voice. It was our man, again, and this time he was hollering,

"Well, Leo, I guess we were *both* wrong." I couldn't help looking at Leo, and he was fighting a grin just as hard as he could.

Another reason that I remember that particular day, I think, was that the fan was doing something that I think every grandstand manager should try. He was taking the *first* guess. I'm not knocking second guesses, I'm just saying that taking the first one is more fun. You might be wrong a little more often, but you'll get a better idea of the satisfaction you can get from being right.

To do that, you might have to follow a team more closely than you have time for. But in the course of this book, you should get some ideas that don't require any more than paying attention to the particular game you're watching. Sometimes, if you and the manager don't see eye to eye, there may be a reason that you don't know about.

Let me give you an example. It was back in the days when Clem Labine was the big man in the Dodgers' bullpen. What a pitcher he was, too! If you're looking for a good relief pitcher, there are certain things you want. He should be strong, so that he can work frequently. Labine was strong. He should be fearless, because when you send for him, you're in trouble. Labine was fearless. As for his pitches, you look for a guy who's either got the overpowering fast ball, for the strikeout, or the real good curve, for the ground ball that can make for double plays. Labine's strengths were a curve and a sinker, and excellent control of both.

Anyway, there came a ball game one day, and while it was a close one, Labine wasn't used. The Dodgers lost in the ninth, and another of our relievers was charged with the defeat. After the game, the press were in the manager's office, discussing the game with Charley Dressen. Finally, one of them said, "Charley, why is Labine in your doghouse?" Charley just looked at him. The writer went on, "If he wasn't in your doghouse, you would have used him today." Charley just kept on staring, and finally said, "Why don't you ask Labine why I didn't use him?"

Gil Hodges (catcher) listens as Manager Leo Durocher gives final instructions to pitcher Rex Barney.

Casey Stengel, the Mets' first manager, gives some advice to the Mets' new manager, Gil Hodges.

I guess the writer took it as a challenge, because he did just that. He walked over to Clem's locker, and said: "You haven't pitched in six days, yet Dressen didn't use you today. Do you have an explanation for that?" Labine spun around and said, "I haven't pitched *in a game* in six days. What you don't realize is that I've warmed up, and warmed up hard, every day for the last six days. My arm is tired. Too tired to pitch today. That's why Dressen didn't use me."

I think that is the kind of thing that a grandstand manager might overlook occasionally. Pitchers can get tired throwing in the bullpen, too. If you're a regular at the ball park, or in front of your radio or television, keep it in mind. If you keep a score-card, make sure that there's room on it for notes, and jot down who's warming up, and for how long. It might explain why a manager isn't using your favorite relief man in a certain spot. It also might show you when the manager is overworking certain pitchers. That happens, too.

Every time a new face shows up among the major-league managers, the question is always asked, "Who will you pattern yourself after?" It was asked of me, and it will be asked of all the new managers to come.

I was very fortunate in the managers that I played for. Leo Durocher, Burt Shotton, Charley Dressen, and Walter Alston with the Dodgers, and Casey Stengel with the Mets. There was another, too. His name was John FitzPatrick, and you might remember him as a coach for the Pittsburgh Pirates when Fred Haney was the manager. Fitz was our manager at Newport News, and he was just great. We were all kids, and what we needed most was patience and encouragement. Fitz gave us both, and some laughs along with the rest. It wouldn't be fair to talk about my managers without mentioning him.

Of the rest, I spent the least time with Leo. I was with him very briefly in 1943. I've told you about how he started me at first base in 1948. In July of that year, Leo made baseball history by switching to the Giants, and replacing Mel Ott. Though I was with him a short time, Durocher had an effect on me, I'm sure. If a player was with Leo for one day, Durocher had to have an effect.

Leo was a daring manager. He'd take chances, and sometimes they'd work, and sometimes they wouldn't. But, more than any manager I ever knew, Leo was the guy that other managers managed against. I've seen managers who'd ignore Leo's team, trying to stay one jump ahead of Leo. It didn't work. One thing that I learned from Durocher is not to try to manage against the other guy. I try to concentrate on running my team, and try to concentrate on stopping only the obvious moves that the other manager might make. If I try to figure out all the things he might possibly do, in every situation, I'm going to lose sight of my own job, and also I'm not giving enough credit to my players.

Burt Shotton was a different type from Durocher in all ways. He was an older man when he took over the Dodgers, and he never wore a uniform. Because of that, he never went out to change a pitcher or argue with an umpire. He never got off that bench from the time the game started until it ended. He was a soft-spoken man, but he knew how to reach a player with his sharp tongue. It helped some players, and didn't help others. But, as far as lessons are concerned, the thing I think that I learned from Shotton was to have confidence in my coaches. He had good ones, and he went along with them. He was very close to his coaches, and relied on them. They, in turn, did a great job for him.

Charley Dressen was probably more like Durocher than any of the others, yet he was very different in a lot of ways. Charley was criticized a lot because of his use of the word "I." I'm not going to try to tell you that he didn't use it a lot. But when I look back at Charley Dressen, I have to realize that Brooklyn was a very special part of his life, and that had an effect on the overall picture.

First of all, Charley managed a lot of clubs in his time, but the Dodgers were his favorites. In later years, he managed the Senators, the Braves, and the Tigers, and fellows who played for him have told me about how Charley would get under their skins with his constant talk about "the way we did it with the Dodgers." They didn't care about the way he did it with the Dodgers, and I don't blame them.

Also, Charley's use of his favorite pronoun was annoying to a lot of people because we were winning. Charley would be saying, "I did this . . ." or "I did that . . ." and people resented it because it sounded like he was taking bows. All I can say to that it that Charley talked the same way when he was managing clubs that were fighting to stay out of the cellar. It was just his way.

Charley was all baseball. He was like Casey Stengel that way. If you wanted to talk baseball, Charley was available twenty-four hours a day. He had theories on every part of the game, and he'd be glad to discuss them with you, too. But as dedicated as he was, Charley also knew how to laugh, even at himself.

I remember, when he first joined us, he brought Cookie Lavagetto along as his number one coach. They had been together in Oakland of the Pacific Coast League. During that time, I guess Charley had tried a lot of his theories, and when he joined the Dodgers, one of his favorite remarks was "That's the way we did it in Oakland. Right, Cookie?"

One day, in Brooklyn, we won a game, but Pee Wee Reese had made an error in the ninth inning. It didn't mean a thing in the outcome of the game. But after the game, Pee Wee was sitting in front of his locker, when Charley Di Giovanna walked up to him. Now Charley was the bat boy, but unlike any bat boy I've ever known. He was a dandy, and I can honestly say that the players on our club really loved Charley.

The best proof of that, I think, came when Charley died sud-

Hodges with manager Bert Shotton after a doubleheader victory.

Manager Chuck Dressen and First Baseman Gil Hodges work out indoors at the Crescent Health Club in Brooklyn before spring training outdoors can begin.

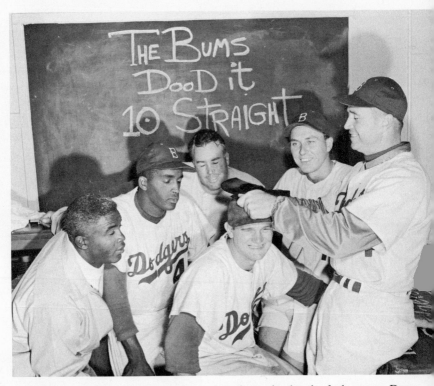

Manager Walter Alston breaks a record on the head of shortstop Don Zimmer, who had four for four this day. That was because that day the Dodgers broke a record for winning their tenth straight game at the opening of the season. From the left, Jackie Robinson, Joe Black, Duke Snider, Gil Hodges.

denly in California. The Dodgers, and ex-Dodgers who knew him, raised a little over $5,000 for his family in the space of a couple of weeks.

But back to the story. Pee Wee is sitting in front of his locker, and Charley walks over. He says: "Pee Wee, you didn't make that play right in the ninth inning. You've got to get in front of the ball like this, then bend down like this, then grab it like this. That's the way we used to do it in Oakland. Right, Cookie?" Well, the whole ball club broke up, because while Charley was doing his imitation of Dressen, Dressen was standing behind him watching it. Nobody laughed harder than Dressen.

It's tough to pinpoint exactly what I learned from Charley Dressen, because there were so many things. But I know what I *hope* I learned from him. I hope I learned that I should always take the job seriously, but never take myself too seriously.

Walter Alston taught me one of the most important things about managing. He taught me that no matter how tough the criticism gets, the job has to be done the way you think it should be done. Alston got more than his share of criticism from the press. He got it from a few of his players. But he also got the job done. Managers talk about "my kind of a ball club." That means that they like to have clubs that play their kind of baseball. Maybe it's power baseball; maybe it's pitching; maybe it's running. But they talk about the kind of club that they have to have. Alston has won pennants with clubs that had lots of power, and with clubs that had next to none. He's won with pitching staffs that were outstanding, and with staffs that were a good deal less than that. He's won with speed, and without it. But he's won, and for major-league managers, that's the name of the game. (It's not the name of the game for all managers, but we'll get around to that later.)

I'm really not in a position to judge Casey Stengel as a manager, as much as I'd like to. I can tell you something about the kind of man he was when I played for him, and that's a big part of any manager. But managing skills don't mean anything if the players can't execute. I played for Casey in the formative years of the Mets, and the players couldn't execute.

I guess you could call the original Mets a club of prospects and reputations. Unfortunately, the prospects were in the future and the reputations were in the past. The Mets were a bad ball club, and I'm one of the reasons that they were a bad club. You hear all the jokes about Marv Throneberry, well, remember that Throneberry played while I sat on the bench.

Speaking of Throneberry, I'd like to say one thing about him. He was proof that losing and making mistakes can be a disease. Once it starts, it's tough to stop. Someday ask Ralph Houk who was the best-looking minor-league ballplayer he ever saw. He'll tell you that it was Throneberry. Maybe if he'd gotten a shot with a different kind of club than the Mets, one where there wasn't pressure on every player all the time, he might have been a success. When I talk about that pressure, I mean it. Losing can build up just as much pressure on a player as winning, and we'll talk about that later, too.

But getting back to Casey: he took a lot of the pressure off the Mets players, particularly the kids. The newspapermen would go to him after somebody blew a game, and instead of rapping the kid, Casey would talk about the good old days in Kankakee. He might chew the player out in the clubhouse, but he never hung him in public.

As an older player, and a guy with a bad knee to boot, I was a liability to Casey for most of my time with him. I was a throwback to the days when the National League was in its glory in New York, and my reputation had to present some problems to Casey.

Yet, his treatment of me was something that I'll never forget. I hope that when I find myself in the same spot someday, I'll remember his thoughtfulness.

But up to now we've talked about me as a manager, and the

managers that I've played for. The idea of this book, though, is
to talk about you as a manager. So let's do that.

Just as all managers are different, so are all managing jobs.
If you're the manager of a Little League team, your job is easier
than mine in certain ways, and in other ways it's harder. The
same thing goes for the high school or college coach. Whether
you have a crack team in the American Legion Junior Baseball
Program, or whether you're managing the Married Men against
the Single Men at the office picnic, you've got problems that I
have, and some that I don't have. The idea of this book is to go
over some of those problems, as well as the fine points of baseball,
from a player's and manager's point of view, so that you, as a
spectator, player, or manager, will understand the game better
and enjoy it more.

MANAGERS

Primary Rule: One Set of Rules

BEFORE I EVER managed my first major-league game, I got one piece of advice that I want to pass on to every manager. Whether you're managing a bunch of six-year-olds in a schoolyard or a major-league ball club, one thing is important above all others. Don't give your players the opportunity to say, "How many sets of rules are there on this club?"

Let's suppose that you're getting ready for your first managing assignment. You sit down and work out a set of rules that you expect your players to obey. When you're through, you might even feel pretty proud of yourself for the fine job you've done. Well, you've just completed the easiest—and most dangerous—job in managing.

It's dangerous because the worst possible thing you can do is make a rule that you're not going to enforce. If you make it, you

Manager Gil gives instructions to relief pitcher Ron Taylor.

Manager Gil gives batting instructions to Ken Singleton.

At spring training: Gil Hodges, J. C. Martin, Al Weis, Al Jackson.

can be pretty sure that somebody's going to test you on it. When they do, you've got to be ready to move. Unfortunately, the guy who tests you may not be the one you expect to do it. Let's say, for example, that it's your Number One pitcher, and you've got a big game coming up. You don't want to upset him.

You decide that you'll overlook it just this once. Your players are watching. They're going to find out who's really running the team. If he gets away with it, you've answered their question. From there on, you can count on your rules being broken a lot more often than your bats.

In professional baseball, the problem is easier to solve than it is at the other levels. If a player is being paid for his services, and he chooses to break a rule, the manager can reach into the player's wallet. If the player is an amateur, the problem gets a little stickier.

Let's stop for a minute and take a look at how fines work. There are a lot of different theories on fining players. There have been managers who didn't believe in it, but most of them find that it's about the only weapon they have.

Eddie Stanky believes that fines can be used to keep the players alert. Eddie will announce in spring training that players who fail to do the proper thing will be fined automatically. The money will be put in the kitty, and the players will have a party with that money when the season is over. It might be any one of a number of things that could result in a fine. For example, the first man up in an inning doubles. The next batter is expected to move that runner over to third. If he doesn't, the fine might be, say, $10.

On the other side of the coin, you find Leo Durocher. Leo doesn't believe in things like $10 fines. He might warn a player a few times, then—*pow*. He once explained his theory by saying, "When I fine a player, he's going to know he's been fined. I believe in starting at $250. I don't ever want to fine a player who can just reach in his pocket and pay it."

My own theory is that I'm reluctant to fine players for their actions on the field, and never for physical mistakes. Mental mistakes, yes. Here's what I mean. One out, and the other team has a man on third base. The batter hits a fly ball to left field. The left fielder drops the ball. To me, that doesn't call for a fine. But suppose the left fielder catches the ball, puts his head down, and jogs in from the outfield, thinking there were two out. The run scores. Do I fine a player of mine who does that? I not only do; I did.

It's happened to me. Not only that, but the run he allowed to score tied up the game, and we lost it in extra innings. It's not reasonable for me to think that any player will catch every ball that is hit to him. But it is reasonable for me to expect that every player on the field knows how many outs have been made in the inning.

I specify things that happen *on* the field, because I'm not so lenient with things that happen off the field. Curfews are a good example. On the road, I expect every player to be in his room two and a half hours after a night game. It's a rule, and if he breaks it, he can expect to lose some of his money. The same thing goes for missing a plane or getting to the ball park late. There are excuses why these things can happen, and I'll listen to those excuses. But they'd better be good. Even more important, they'd better be true.

The reasons are simple. I don't consider that it's my job to supervise the morals or the habits of my players. These men are professionals. If I was managing a team of youngsters, it might be a different story. But my players are supposed to be men. They are also supposed to be in shape to do their jobs. Rest is an important ingredient in doing the job. If they're going to stay out all night, they're hurting the ball club, and my job is to see that they don't hurt the club. If I let them get away with breaking the rules, I'm inviting the others to do the same thing.

I'm not going to try to tell you that in my experience as a

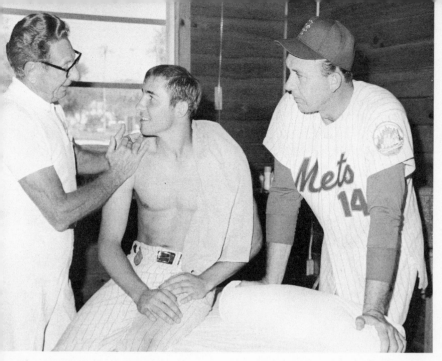

The manager watches as the trainer, Gus Mauch, massages Ken Boswell's shoulder.

Manager Hodges and General Manager John Murphy watch batting practice.

manager, no player has ever gotten away with violating the curfew. Sure they have. But only because I didn't know about it. It's the risk they run, and the players know it. When they're caught out, or miss a plane, they expect to be fined.

In spring training one year, I was standing across the street from the hotel when I saw four of my players leave. It was about ten minutes before curfew. I hung around for a half hour, and they didn't come back. The next day, in the clubhouse, I made a little speech. I told the club that I knew that some of the players had broken curfew, and I was going to give them an opportunity to save some money. If they wanted to pay $50 fines right now, the case would be closed. If the money wasn't in by the end of the day, I'd hold another meeting, and name names. The only thing was that the fines would then be $100 apiece.

I told them they could leave their checks on the desk in my office. About an hour later, Joe Pignatano, one of my coaches, walked over to where I was hitting fungoes. He had a great big grin on his face. He said: "You made a smart move. You offered four guys a chance to admit they broke curfew, but you'd better put a guard on the door of your office. Seven guys have paid the fine already."

Let me say something here about the habits of ballplayers. It has been my experience, ever since I started playing, that most players live by the rules. It's the old story: You hear about the ones who break them, but not about the guys who keep them. I would have to say that the behavior record of major-league ballplayers, all things considered, is outstanding. When I say "all things considered," I mean that they are usually young men, away from home, and earning good money, with plenty of opportunities to break the rules. Still, their record in that area is outstanding.

However, the manager of a team that isn't professional has only one other recourse. If the player breaks rules, on or off the field, the only action the manager has is to keep the player on the

An array of stars, past, present, and future, at Shea Stadium. Standing, from the left, present pitching star Nolan Ryan, former stars Sandy Koufax, Pee Wee Reese, Gil Hodges. Seated in front is Sal Visone, pitcher for Gil Hodges's Little League team, and Sidney S. Loberfeld, counsel to the Little League and to Gil Hodges.

bench. Which gets me back to my original premise: If you're not prepared to keep *every* player who breaks a rule on the bench, then you'd better not put in the rule.

Speaking of the bench, let's take a look at it right now. It's an important part of managing any team. The morale, the discipline, the attitude of a team are all reflected on the bench. It's part of the manager's job to keep a constant watch on all these things. The younger the players, the more important it is for the manager to be on the bench. If he's coaching at third base, it's true he can give the signs better. But there a lot more problems that need his attention on the bench.

For one thing, you must consider the players themselves. Usually, it's better to let criticism wait at least until after the game, and preferably until the next day. But there is sound, constructive advice that can be given between innings. Also, a youngster who's had a bad inning in the field might need a little encouraging.

If your team is behind, somebody has to try to keep the hope of winning alive. In this respect, the baseball manager has a problem that's unique. Unlike a football team or a basketball team, a baseball team is never so far behind that it can't catch up. The clock is not a factor. Realistically, chances of victory might be very slim; but the thing to remember, and the thing for you to see that your players remember, is that those chances do exist. There's nothing more rewarding to a ball club, in many ways, than winning a game that looked like it was lost.

Again, getting back to the conduct of a bench, the younger the team, the more important it is that the manager keep a check on them. A lively, spirited bench is desirable. An abusive, nasty bench is a reflection on the players, their upbringing, and, especially, the manager. He should stop it, and if he doesn't, or can't, then he's kidding himself if he thinks he's really managing that team.

Encourage your players to encourage their teammates. You

have to channel the interest of the players who aren't playing, and those interests should be channeled into something constructive. It is much more important that they support their own team than it is to have them being abusive to the other team.

There are several reasons for this, and one of them is a word that sometimes gets abused—"sportsmanship." That doesn't diminish its importance to me. Sportsmanship is a very important part of what a youngster should get out of baseball. A very minute percentage of the young men who play baseball, from Little League through college, will ever play professionally. As a result, it's doubtful that the skills of the game will ever be very valuable to them. But the lessons of teamwork and sportsmanship will be valuable, so it's the duty of a manager to see that his players receive these values.

Another argument against abusing other players is that it doesn't really serve much purpose. Youngsters might be affected, it's true. But that also goes for the youngsters on your own team. To be completely honest about it, most kids overlook it. What can be worst of all is the fact that it makes some fellows better players. There's much to be said for the theory of "Let sleeping dogs lie."

As for abusing umpires, that makes even less sense. A little later on, we'll get around to the pitfalls of that.

Another thing we'll be getting around to later is the subject of Little League baseball. Like a lot of people, I have some criticisms to make. But I also have appreciation for a lot of things that Little League does, and I'd like to point out one of them right here.

In its *Handbook*, Little League has a rule which could well be adopted in all phases of amateur baseball. Rule XIV (*c*) states, "Managers and adult coaches shall not be permitted in the coaching boxes."

Let's take a look at what that can mean to a manager. Most important, it lets him get two more players into every game, and gives these two players a real chance to contribute to their team's efforts. But how much these two players get out of their opportunity depends, to a large extent, on the manager. The manager can make important use of these two players, and here are some suggestions along that line. Remember, please, that I'm talking about every kind of team other than a professional one.

First, a manager should rotate his coaches, if he's drawing them from the ranks of his players. Give everyone an opportunity to try his hand. Some might be better than others, but you might get fooled on who's a good coach and who isn't. Also, the decision of who will be coaching on a certain day should not be made at the last minute, if that's avoidable.

The coaches should be instructed to pay particular attention to the practice session of the other team. Who are the power hitters on the other team? Which outfielders have strong arms, and which have weak arms? How does the catcher throw? It's to be expected that the coach is familiar with the talents of his own players.

Now the coach is in a position to be a positive force on his team. Let's suppose that there's a man on second base, and the batter gets a base hit. The coach, knowing that the ball has been hit to an outfielder with a weak arm, waves the runner around third. A run scores, and it proves to be the winning run. A player who didn't play contributed to a victory, and any manager should be pleased with that. If the manager himself was coaching, and waved that runner around, the run wouldn't mean the same thing to the team.

Having taken care of the two extra men, now it's time to give some thought to the ones who are going to play. You're the manager. Part of your job is to make out the lineup and the batting order. What are the things for you to take into consideration?

Before we break the offensive and defensive lineup down by position, there's one thing you should look for above all else.

Desire. Does he *want* to play? Desire can overcome a lot of things. Desire alone can't do the job, but if he hasn't got desire, the talent can be an awful waste.

Desire has made players, and lack of desire has ruined them. Leo Durocher once described Eddie Stanky as a guy who "couldn't hit, couldn't run, couldn't throw, but could beat you." Stanky had talent, or he wouldn't have gotten to the big leagues. But, even more, he had desire; otherwise he wouldn't have stayed in the big leagues.

I once had a catcher, and I'd heard before we made the deal that he "didn't like to play." That's the way baseball people describe the lack of desire. It's a bad rap to put on a player, and one that spreads very quickly. Anyway, that's the kind of reputation that this fellow had.

He was out for a while with injuries, and, finally, the team physician told me that he couldn't find anything more wrong with the player. As far as the doctor could tell, the fellow was ready to play. I still let him rest for another week or so, because he complained occasionally.

Finally, we were in a game that was very close. I wanted to use a pitch hitter for the guy who was catching, so I walked over to the fellow who'd been hurt. I said to him, "Can you give me a couple of innings behind the plate? I'd like to hit for this guy, and see if we can get something going." He looked up and said, "Sorry."

Right then I knew that the scouting reports had been right. He didn't want to play. At the time we got him, I was surprised that he'd been available. Now I knew why. I made up my mind I'd never ask him again. When it came time to get rid of him, I found out that nobody was interested. They already knew what I'd found out the hard way.

One of the advantages of making out an imaginary lineup, as opposed to a real one, is that you can use your imagination. So, for our purposes, all your players have desire. Congratulations.

Now, one more thing. The approach of a manager who's going to run a Little League or a sandlot or a high school or a college team is basically different from that of the major-league manager. One is positive, and the other is negative. My job is to make out a lineup of professional players. Men who've had an opportunity to learn the skills of their various positions. Men who've proved, during a period of apprenticeship, that they can handle the duties of their position.

Also, if I find myself with too many infielders, and not enough catchers, then I can make a trade. We have to assume that you're not in either of these positions. You're going to have to make do with what you've got. I can approach the problem positively, while you must approach it negatively. You've got to make a team out of what you've got, so let's see how we might go about it.

First, take the left-handed throwers. From these, you can come up with a first baseman and three outfielders. That is, your first baseman and your outfielders *can* be left-handed. They don't have to be, but the left-handers can't play the other infield spots, and they can't catch.

There are a lot of theories on why this is true. There have been a few left-handed catchers, very few. I would forget about a left-handed catcher for one simple reason. Having a special glove made for him can be very expensive. As for the infield spots, I really feel that a right-handed thrower is in a better position to make the plays. (If you want a pleasant picture to think about, imagine a left-handed second baseman pivoting for the double play.)

If you're starting from scratch, here's one method. Work out all your infielders at shortstop. The one with the best range should wind up playing shortstop, providing he has the arm to play there.

As the players get older, the necessity of a strong arm in the infield lessens. I'm not knocking strong-armed infielders, I'm just saying that there are other things more important than the

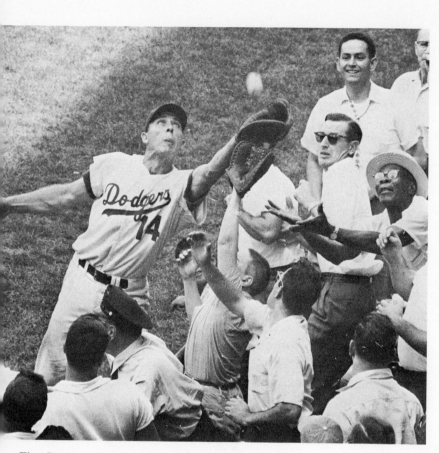

First Baseman Hodges snares a foul at Ebbets Field.

A fielding sequence in the Dodgers–White Sox World Series game at Los Angeles Coliseum. The White Sox have the bases loaded. Upper left: Billy Goodman hits a slow roller toward Hodges. Upper right: He fields it and waits to tag Goodman. Lower left: Goodman tries to evade the tag out. Lower right: Hodges tags him out. In the background, Second Baseman Charley Neal.

strength of the arm. The best example of that, in my time, was Phil Rizzuto. Phil didn't have a great arm. In fact, it was below average. But he was still one of the greatest of all shortstops. He made up for his arm by getting rid of the ball very quickly. It's good to remember that the fastest runner in the world can't outrun the ball.

But while the strength of the arm might not be all-important, the accuracy is. An erratic arm is at least twice as bad as a weak one. If the throw is weak, the runner may reach first safely. If it's wild, the runner will probably wind up on second.

The quickest hands should be playing third base. The cliché in baseball is, "At third base, you do or you don't." It means that the ball is hit down there so hard usually that the third baseman only gets one chance at the ball. He comes up with it or he doesn't. Speed isn't necessarily a qualification at third base, but the arm does enter into it. Because the third baseman may have to hold the ball, waiting for the first baseman to reach the bag, he has plenty of time to set himself for the throw.

At second base, you should put your fastest infielder, because he really has a lot of ground to cover. In addition to second base, there are a lot of plays where he's required to cover first. A lazy second baseman can kill you. A good one will back up the shortstop sometimes, and also the first baseman sometimes. He spends a lot of time serving as a cut-off man in the outfield. He also has to do one of the single toughest things on the field, pivot on the double play. The quicker he can reach second base and set himself, the easier that pivot play is for him to make.

In the outfield, the man with the best range should be your center fielder. That doesn't necessarily mean the most speed. A big factor in determining the range of an outfielder is his ability to get a jump on the ball. The importance of the center fielder's arm is determined by the ball park you're playing in.

During the early 1950's, there were three teams playing in New York City. The fans of the different teams used to argue about which player had the best man at each position, but the hottest arguments concerned center fielder. The Dodgers had Duke Snider; the Giants had Willie Mays; and the Yankees had Mickey Mantle. They were all great ballplayers, and all outstanding power hitters. But in the outfield, each one had something he did better than the others.

Mantle had the greatest speed. He looked like he could outrun the ball. Center field in the stadium was big, and Mickey broke the hearts of a lot of hitters by catching "uncatchable" drives. Mays was also capable of covering a lot of ground, but the thing he did best was field balls hit in front of him. I don't mean fly balls; I mean ground balls. He charged them like an infielder, and that ability, plus a great arm, cut down a lot of base runners.

In Brooklyn, center field was nowhere near as big an area to cover as it was in the other two parks. But Snider had no equal in playing the center-field fence. He would literally run up the fence to catch balls, and he knew every possible carom that the ball might take.

The point is that the proper answer to which of the three was the best center fielder, was, in my opinion, that each of them was the best in his home park. Each was ideally suited for the park he was playing in.

Having determined your center fielder, your next move is to find the strongest arm and put it in right field. No great mystery about that. Your right fielder might have to throw to home or to third, and your left fielder won't have to throw to first. Hence, the stronger arm belongs in right field.

For catching, we get back to desire. *I* can *demand* certain things from a catcher. *You* can only *ask* for volunteers. I don't really know why youngsters are reluctant to catch. It's harder work, maybe, but it's also more interesting. In any case, there's no need for me to list a lot of qualifications for a catcher. Your job is to find a kid who wants to catch. The only clue I might give you is that speed is less important to a catcher than to any other player.

I haven't forgotten first base; I've just saved it for last. You watch your infielders throw, then determine how important a first baseman is to you. If they've all got accurate arms, the first baseman is determined by the way he swings the bat. If you've got scatter-arm infielders, you'd better make sure your first baseman is a guy who can move around the bag, and dig the ball out of the dirt.

In Little League ball, the game is often dominated by the pitcher. He might strike out fourteen or fifteen men a game. In that case, the importance of the defense is negligible. But, other than that, it's wise to remember that the team that makes the fewest mistakes is usually going to win. Defense is every bit as important as offense.

I haven't mentioned pitchers here because they're worth a chapter all by themselves.

As for the batting order, you have several things to remember. I would say, as a rule of thumb, have your fastest runner lead off. The man with the best bat control should bat second. Your three best hitters should bat third, fourth, and fifth. Of your remaining three hitters, the one with the best power should bat sixth, and the one with the best speed should bat eighth. The reason for putting a fast man in the eighth spot, among other things, is that you don't want the pitcher hitting into a double play, if it can be avoided. Even more important, especially at the higher levels of baseball, it's likely that you'll have the pitcher bunting if there are less than two out.

Yours is a hard job, but at all phases of the amateur level, part of that job is to see that your players enjoy the game. For them, the game is supposed to be fun. If it's fun for them, it should be fun for you, too.

Don't try to be a genius, especially if you're working with kids. If you're working with professionals, you still shouldn't try to be a genius. Sometimes it's difficult for a manager to realize how important or unimportant his job is.

The late Larry Goetz, a great umpire, was once criticized by a writer because Goetz had thrown Durocher out of one game of a double-header, and Frank Frisch out of the other game. The writer complained to Goetz that the fans wanted to see these managers. Goetz gave him an answer that all of us managers would do well to remember.

Larry said: "Let me tell you something. When Honus Wagner was a little boy, he lived twelve miles from the Pittsburgh ball park. He used to walk there every day, climb up to the top of a big tree behind the left-field fence, and watch the game. When it was over, he would climb back down, and walk home. Now, do you think that boy would really walk twenty-four miles, and climb up and down a tree, just to see somebody manage?"

Pictured above are the top brass of the Mets (left to right): John J. Murphy, Vice-President and General Manager; G. Herbert Walker, Jr., member of the Board of Directors; M. Donald Grant, Chairman of the Board of Directors; Joan W. Payson, President; Frederick K. Trask, Jr., member of the Board of Directors; George M. Weiss, member of the Board of Directors; James K. Thomson, Vice-President and Business Manager.

PITCHERS
Primary Rule: Keep 'em Moving

IF I WAS a psychologist, I could probably tell you why it is that pitchers are different from the rest of the men on a ball club. But I'm not a psychologist; I'm a baseball man. As a result, I don't know why they're different, but I know that they are.

Maybe it's because they don't get to play every day; maybe it's because they're more dependent on the other players; or maybe it's because the eventual victory or defeat is charged to them. Whatever it is, managers have to learn to live with it.

Not only are pitchers different from the other players; they're usually different from other pitchers. Each one can present a different problem to a manager, and to the coach who's in charge of the pitchers.

Let's take the simple matter of whether or not a pitcher is

49

going to start a game. There are some guys who like to know. They like to prepare themselves mentally and physically for the job. There are others who are worriers, and the manager doesn't tell them that they're starting until the last possible moment.

Last season, for example, Denny McLain, of the Tigers, knew his pitching assignments from the middle of August until the end of the season. By that I mean that on August 15th, McLain could tell you every time he would pitch from then until the end of the season. Now, I admit that McLain's case was unusual. The Tigers had a pretty good lead, and McLain was trying to become the first thirty-game winner since 1934. But the point is that McLain wasn't affected by knowing when he would pitch.

On the other hand, I've been on clubs with pitchers who would lie awake all night if they knew that they were going to start the next day. If a manager knows that his pitcher might react that way, he just waits until the pitcher gets to the clubhouse, and then lets him know. Sometimes the pitcher learns that he's the starter by walking to his locker and finding a brand-new baseball in his baseball shoe.

That's a baseball tradition, but I would advise managers not to use it. One practical joker, plus a half-dozen baseballs, and you can wind up with six guys, all convinced that they're going to start today's game.

Sometimes managers find that the plotting and planning that they do to come up with the right pitcher in a certain game all winds up meaning nothing. Leo Durocher once found that out with a pretty good left-hander, Dave Koslo.

In those days, the Cardinals were loaded with good left-handed hitters, and the Dodgers had a great bunch of right-handed hitters. The managers of the other teams tried to have their lefties ready for the Cardinals, and their right-handed pitching set for Brooklyn.

Now, Leo used to have a pet expression about pitching. He used to say: "Pitch today's pitcher today. It may rain tomorrow."

President Lyndon B. Johnson and Gil with other greats at the opening day of the 1966 season at D.C. Stadium. Vice-President Humphrey is behind Johnson. Speaker McCormack and Stan Musial are at the President's right; Senator Mansfield, Baseball Commissioner Ford C. Frick, Gil Hodges, Bill Rigney, George Selkirk, and Joe Cronin are gathered around the President.

What he meant, of course, was use the pitcher who was ready, and not try to save him for a spot. Leo was doomed to have his theory backfire on him, just as theories have backfired on everybody who ever managed a ball club, and that includes me.

Anyway, Leo held Koslo out of a turn to have him ready for the Cardinals. Durocher was managing the Giants at the time, and it was a year when it was especially important for him to beat the contenders, as the Cardinals and the Dodgers were. He started planning for the Cardinals series about two weeks in advance, and he tried to move Koslo around so that he'd be ready. Well, he caught a couple of rainouts along the way, and one day Koslo was sick, and by the time the Giants got to St. Louis, Koslo had had eleven days' rest. I think the Cardinals knocked him out by the third inning.

Just last year, I found myself in a spot. The Mets had come up with some good young pitchers, and I had five good starters at the time. But what with doubleheaders and extra-inning games, I found myself without a starter who had enough rest. We were playing the Cincinnati Reds, without question the best hitting team in baseball.

I decided to go to my bullpen, and get Cal Koonce. Now, Cal had been outstanding for me in relief, but he hadn't started a game in over a year. I told him that I was hoping he could give us five good innings, and then I'd get him some help. Bear in mind that five innings was the most Koonce had worked all year, and it was now almost Labor Day.

My thinking was that if we could just stay close, we'd have a chance. Koonce gave up exactly one hit in the first six innings, and we managed to come up with two runs. The first man up in the seventh got a hit, and Koonce struck out the next man, but he was obviously getting tired. I brought in Ron Taylor from the bullpen, and Taylor got the next eight men in a row, and we won 2–0. One of the best pitched games of the year, and I had it forced on me, because I had nobody else to pitch.

On the subject of starting pitchers, managers have been known to have different ideas about picking spots for certain men. As an example, let's suppose that two teams are going to play each other and both of them are ready to start their Number One pitcher. Some managers feel that they should hold out their Number One man, and pitch him the next day, the idea being that Number One is more likely to win if he's not hooked up with another Number One.

It's a theory that I don't go along with. I believe in keeping my rotation going as much as possible. If the rotation calls for my top pitcher to go against the other club's top pitcher today, then that's the way it'll be. Maybe tomorrow, my Number Four goes against their Number Four, but I'm still not going to hold out my best man to pitch against their Number Four. I might lose twice or I might get a split, but I feel that I have to take the position that I might win twice. That's still the name of the game.

This doesn't mean that I would never break my rotation. I've done it, and I'll do it again, but not for that reason. Certain clubs wear out certain pitchers, and part of managing is to try to avoid that. Certainly one of the best pitchers in baseball history was Warren Spahn, yet we didn't see much of him when I was with the Dodgers. That was especially true when the Braves came to Brooklyn.

It made sense. Spahn was a left-hander who had to pitch against a lineup that was almost exclusively right-handed hitting. As a matter of fact, we saw very little left-handed pitching in those years. Spahn didn't care much for the theory, but, as a manager, I can understand it. It's merely that the type of pitcher that Spahn was made the Dodgers a very rough club for him. If I had a pitcher like Spahn on my team—please—I'd probably handle things the same way.

Spahn was an ideal pitcher, in a lot of ways. He helped himself defensively; he was a good hitter and a good base runner. But, mostly, he had the ideal outlook for a pitcher. He didn't rattle easily, and he worked everything out very carefully before a game. He knew exactly what he wanted to do with each batter, and he knew how he intended to go about doing it.

Lew Burdette, another great pitcher, roomed with Spahn in those days, and he described Spahnie's approach to pitching by saying: "My roomie can't have too much fun while he's pitching, because he's too busy making plans. While he's pitching to the second man up in the first inning, he's already figuring out what to do with the third man up in the fifth inning."

Actually, it wasn't that bad, but Spahn tried to lay out his whole game before it started. His record shows you how well it worked. However, Spahn was Spahn, and most pitchers don't have either his talent or his powers of concentration.

Temper, or temperament, can be a tremendous factor to a pitcher. Controlling his temper can be much more important than controlling his fast ball. The reason is simple. If a pitcher loses his temper, he also loses his powers of reasoning, and that's a luxury that pitchers can afford less than anybody else on the field.

The pitcher makes a decision before he throws the ball. The batter must react. The defensive players must react in turn, if the batter hits the ball. But the pitcher is not reacting until after he throws the ball. Before he throws it, he's planning. He must decide if the pitch will be a fast ball or a curve or a change of pace or whatever pitches he might have. He must decide whether the ball will be inside or outside, high or low.

On that subject, let me point out that the catcher doesn't tell the pitcher what to throw, in most cases. He suggests. Where the pitcher is very young, and the catcher is a veteran, that might not always be true. But for the most part, a pitcher pitches his own game. He's got to throw the ball to the best of his ability, and to do that he must believe that the pitch is the right one. Managers don't want to hear pitchers come back to the bench and say, "I didn't want to throw that pitch in that spot, but he called for it." That's why the good Lord gave pitchers necks, so they can shake off catchers.

But getting back to tempers, I've seen some pitchers in my time who really hurt themselves with their tempers. Billy Loes pitched in Brooklyn while I was there, and I guess Billy will be remembered for a lot of things other than his pitching. (It was Loes who said he didn't want to be a twenty-game winner, because then he'd be expected to do it every year. It was also Loes who picked the Yankees to win a World Series one year. There were two things wrong with that. First, the Yankees were playing the Dodgers in that Series. Second, he was right.)

Loes, because of his temper, will never be appreciated for his talent. He was a pitcher who had everything, including an excellent idea of how to pitch. But when an umpire called pitches on Loes that Billy didn't agree with, his temper took over. He tried to throw the ball harder than he really could. He lost sight of the fact that he was trying to set up a hitter for a certain pitch.

When things were going right for Billy, it was a wonderful feeling to know that he was on your side. But when he got upset, he would start to walk around the mound in big circles. When he started those long walks, we all knew we were in trouble.

When the subject of bad-tempered pitchers comes up, I guess there's no question that my nomination for the champ has to be Russ Meyer. The "Mad Monk" was a good pitcher, too. He hung around the big leagues a long time, and pitched for several pennant-winning teams. He was a nice guy, too, with a good sense of humor, and always willing to do someone a favor.

But when the game started, he was all business. He was a tough competitor, which is an asset for a pitcher. But when he blew his top, it was like plugging a hose into an electric socket. Most of the time, the other fellows on the team would be upset about the same things, so the humor of the situation wasn't appreciated until later. But one day, it was impossible for anybody to keep a straight face.

I don't think anyone remembers now what caused Russ to lose his cool, but nobody who was there will ever forget what happened. The Monk started to storm around on the mound, and he was yelling at the same time. Finally, he picked up the rosin bag, and threw it up in the air, as high as he could. Then he stood there, legs apart, hands on his hips, and just hollered at the umpire. Right in the middle of his speech, the rosin bag came down—and hit Meyer right on top of the head.

The worst kinds of outbursts that a pitcher can make are the ones that are directed against his own players. There's no question that a pitcher can be upset when one of his teammates drops a ball, and turns an out into a base run, or even a run. But the pitcher who shows everybody how unhappy he is, who embarrasses the player who made the error, is causing a situation that the manager has to stop, and quickly.

Sometimes it's necessary to point out to a pitcher that if he intends to show his unhappiness when a fielder drops a ball, then maybe the fielders should do the same thing when the pitcher gives up a walk. Fielders don't drop baseballs on purpose, any more than pitchers make bad pitches on purpose. The pitcher who has a tendency to show up his teammates has to be stopped. He destroys the morale of the players behind him, and the fans are all able to see his reaction.

We had a case of it on the Dodgers one time. Don Newcombe, who very rarely ever did anything like that, let everyone in the park know that he was upset when Sandy Amoros dropped a fly ball in left field. There was quite a fuss about it in the papers for a couple of days, and all the players, especially Newk, wished it had never happened.

The next time Newcombe pitched, Amoros hit two home runs over the scoreboard in right field. In the *Daily News* the next day, Dick Young began his story of the game by writing, "Sandy Amoros dropped two fly balls yesterday. Both on Bedford Avenue." Newcombe laughed harder than anybody.

When you talk about pitchers, you have to talk about pitches. The pitch that fascinates the public the most has to be the fast ball. The guy who can rear back and get that little something

President Eisenhower with Gil Hodges and George Selkirk, General Manager of the Senators, in Washington in 1965.

The Mets' Manager Gil Hodges and General Manager John Murphy greet Mrs. Lou Gehrig (left) and Mrs. Babe Ruth during an Old-Timers' Game at Shea Stadium. Hodges wears his "old-time" Dodger uniform.

extra is the one that the customers want to see. Men like Walter Johnson, Bob Feller, Sandy Koufax, and Dizzy Dean are the ones that the public considers the best kind of pitchers to watch.

I don't think that there's any question about the value of the fast ball. It has to be rated as the number one pitch for any pitcher to have. There are several reasons for that. It's easier to control than the others, or should be. It's the most important pitch for a pitcher who's looking to strike a batter out. (I don't mean that a pitcher will always strike a man out with the fast ball, only that the threat of a fast ball makes the batter more liable to strike out.)

An effective part of any pitcher's repertoire is his ability to change speeds, but the slow pitch is effective only if it serves as a change of pace. I've never known a pitcher who could be classiged as great who didn't have a fast ball.

Now, I can imagine that a lot of people will say that Eddie Lopat or Stu Miller didn't have fast balls. Don't you believe it. It might not have been their bread-and-butter pitch, but it was there. About the time that a hitter decided he wasn't going to see a fast ball from one of them, one went right by. It may not have been as fast as the one Koufax threw, but it was just as effective, especially if the umpire said, "Strike three."

One reason that managers look for a fast ball from a young pitcher is that if he doesn't have it, nobody can teach it to him. You can help pitchers to learn to throw curves or sliders or knucklers, but the best you can hope for is that you can help a fast-ball pitcher with his control. If he can't throw hard, making him a winning pitcher is going to be a lot of work.

If the fast ball is the best pitch a pitcher can have, it's also the most dangerous to him. Most good hitters are, primarily, fast-ball hitters. That is, they figure to get more base hits, and even more important, more home runs, off fast balls. The fast ball, with something on it, in the right place, can be the best pitch in the world. A fast ball right over the middle of the plate, at something less than superspeed, can be the worst.

Scientists might convince you that the curve ball is an optical illusion. You—not me. The same guys who tell you they're sure there are flying saucers will tell you there's no such thing as a a curve ball. I know better.

The sharp-breaking curve ball can be the strikeout pitch that the pitcher needs. Or it might be the ball that's hit on the ground and turns into a double play. It can be the difference between being a good pitcher and a great one. Sandy Koufax is the best example I know of that. From the first day he joined the Dodgers, Sandy could throw hard. His problem was control.

When he got control of the fast ball, he became a good pitcher. When he got control of his curve ball, which also was outstanding, he turned the corner to greatness.

The curve ball breaks down and away. The sharp-breaking curve that catches the outside of the plate, knee-high, is as good a pitch as there is. Walter Alston once said: "I've heard of a lot of guys who could always handle that pitch. The only trouble is that I've never seen one. I've seen guys get occasional base hits off it, but I've never seen anybody do it consistently."

Notice that I keep talking about the "sharp-breaking" curve ball. Sometimes a curve ball breaks very slowly. It's known as a hanging curve, and the only thing it's really good for is a hitter's morale. As Dizzy Trout has pointed out, home runs get hit off *good* fast balls, and *good* curves, as well as bad ones. But if you want to see a hitter's eyes light up like a pinball machine, watch him when he sees a hanging curve ball.

The slider is a breaking pitch, like the curve. The difference is that while the slider doesn't break as much as a curve ball, it does break faster. Stan Musial says that the biggest difference in hitting now, as opposed to when he broke in, is the slider. I know that when I started to play, I didn't see many of them. Today, most pitchers have one. It's very effective, because it breaks quickly, quicker than a curve. But it can also hang.

Another thing about the slider is that it's tough on certain pitchers' arms. Since it's a pitch that can be taught, I'd suggest that a youngster who wants to be a professional pitcher leave the slider alone until he can get some advice from a qualified pitching coach. Throwing the slider might make you a winning pitcher. It might also make you an ex-pitcher.

The best way I can describe my feelings about the slider is to say that if a pitcher has, say, three good pitches, then he should forget the slider. If he has a fast ball, a curve, and a change of pace, for example, then he doesn't need the slider. When the time comes that his fast ball has lost something, that's the time to start to work on the slider.

While the idea of pitching is to get the batter out, there are two kinds of pitches that don't fall into that category, in the strict sense, and good pitchers have to know about the value of these pitches.

One is called the "waste" pitch. The idea is that a pitcher who has the count in his favor can afford to throw a pitch that's out of the strike zone. If the batter swings at it, he's swinging at a bad pitch, which is something the pitcher always wants. If the batter doesn't swing, the pitcher is still in control.

The other pitch can be used in the same spot, but it isn't really being wasted. Let's use a specific hitter as an example. The Pittsburgh Pirates' first baseman, Donn Clendenon, has earned the reputation of being a terrific "off-speed" hitter. In other words, throwing him a change of pace can be extremely dangerous. He's proved that to every manager in the National League, including this one.

Now, let's say that your pitcher has a one strike and no balls count on Clendenon. This might be the spot to show him a change-up. Notice that I said *show* it to him, not throw it to him. The difference is that the pitch must be outside the strike zone, maybe where he can't even reach it. If he swings, again you have the advantage of a hitter going for a bad ball. But even if he doesn't swing, the pitch serves a purpose. It helps with your next pitch. If you come back with a fast ball, it looks just a little faster because it comes after a change-up.

Maybe those two pitches sound like the same thing to you, so let me repeat the difference. The "waste" pitch is meant merely for the batter to swing at a bad ball. The other is primarily to set up the hitter for the next pitch.

Now, let's take a look at three of the most publicized pitches in baseball. First, the knuckle ball. The knuckler is not designed to overpower the hitter or even to fool him, really. The basic idea is to frustrate him. The problem is that it frustrates the catcher, too. It's just as hard to catch as it is to hit. There have been a lot of catchers who put on a mask just to warm up a knuckle-ball pitcher in the bullpen.

If you've never seen a knuckle ball, or at least a good one, let me try to describe it. In the first place, it doesn't spin while it's in the air, nor does it usually travel very fast. But it seems to dance on its way to the plate. The air currents seem to make it rise and fall, with no definite pattern.

The knuckler is easy on the arm, as can be proved by the fact that Hoyt Wilhelm is still pitching at forty-five. But it's very difficult to control, and especially tough on catchers. A pitcher who throws a knuckler as his number one pitch should realize from the start that he's at the mercy of catchers. If he winds up on a club that doesn't have a catcher who can handle him, he really isn't going to be very valuable to that club.

The best way to illustrate the problems of the knuckle ball is to describe something that I saw happen in Ebbets Field one day, and I tell you now that if you have trouble believing me, you just have to try, because it's true.

Hoyt Wilhelm was pitching against us that day in a game with the Giants. I think I should point out here that Wilhelm is, without doubt, the best knuckle-ball pitcher I've ever seen, and I don't know anyone in baseball who doesn't feel the same way.

On the day I'm talking about, the Giants' catcher was Ray Noble, a big Cuban, who was known as one of the strongest men in the game. It was the ninth inning, and we had a man on third base. Wilhelm wound up, threw his knuckler, and the batter was fooled. Unfortunately, so was Noble. Maybe the ball "zigged" when it should have "zagged," but whatever happened, it went all the way to the backstop. The runner on third scored easily with the winning run.

Noble was so frustrated that he reached down and grabbed the flap on his shin guards. The flap is the little part that protects the catcher's instep. With a flap in each hand, Noble pulled, and those shin guards came right off in his hands. Remember that there are three straps and clasps on each shin guard, yet Noble just tore his off. That should tell you about Noble's strength, and also about the frustrations of trying to catch a knuckle ball.

Now let's get around to the so-called "mystery" pitch, the spitball. As a hitter, I was opposed to it. As a manager, I'm still opposed to it.

I don't think that there's any area in all baseball that the fan is more misguided about than the spitter. I don't know if I can clear the situation up, but I'm going to try.

First, the spitball was barred in 1920. Pitchers who were then in the major leagues were allowed to throw it, but nobody who came along later would be permitted to use it. Believe it or not, I don't think there has been a real spitball pitcher since those fellows who had the okay finally left the big leagues.

That calls for an explanation. A spitball pitcher in the old days usually chewed a substance called slippery elm. He would apply enough of it on the ball to disturb the center of balance. Then he would wet his fingers and pitch. Like the knuckler, the spitball didn't rotate, and it broke down sharply.

Since those days, a lot of pitchers have wet their fingers before

At the left, Angel Pitcher Jack Hamilton appears to be loading up to throw a spitball, as he had been doing repeatedly during the game. At the right, above, Washington manager Gil Hodges on one of his trips to the plate to protest to the umpires, who repeatedly made ball changes, but Hodges played the game under protest. At lower right, Manager Bill Rigney protests that Hodges and his coaches are harassing Hamilton. The Senators won the game.

they threw. That's illegal, but it's not the same spitball that the old-timers threw. The ball still dips, but nowhere near so much. The main advantage of today's spitballer is that the ball leaves his hand, because of the moisture, in such a way that he can get it to break suddenly.

The public sometimes gets the idea that nobody can hit a spitball, which is ridiculous. The knuckler is much tougher to hit. My objection to the spitter, very simply, is that it's a tough pitch to control. Any pitch is a good one only when the pitcher can get it over. Unless you can throw it consistently for strikes, the spitter, or any other pitch, is a bad one.

There's been a lot written about the spitter, and it's given people the idea that a pitcher who can get away with throwing it is invincible. Let me sum up my feelings this way: It's hard to control, which makes it a bad pitch. I've seen batters strike out on spitballs, and I've seen spitballs wind up as souvenirs for some guy in the bleachers. It's the problem of the people who run baseball to determine whether or not the pitch is illegal. My job is to decide whether it's a good pitch for my pitchers, and my answer is that, almost always, it isn't.

Which brings us around to the pitch with all the different names. It's called the "brushback," the "knockdown," the "duster," and a lot of other names. It's another misunderstood pitch, as far as I'm concerned.

You hear it said, "I've never seen a pitcher throw at a batter deliberately, to hit him." I can't go along with that. I've seen it, as I'll explain later. However, I don't think that I've ever seen a pitcher throw at a batter to *hurt* him. Maybe I'd better use the word "injure" instead of "hurt," because there's no way of getting hit with a baseball that isn't going to hurt.

Some pitchers, who knock down a lot of hitters, get reputations as "headhunters." I don't honestly believe that a pitcher who tries consistently to hit batters is going to stay in the big leagues. In the first place, it's a sign of weakness, not strength. The idea is to get the batter out, not put him on base. If you can't get him out, you're not going to hang around very long.

Another thing to consider is that a "headhunter" isn't going to be very popular with his own teammates. If I have a pitcher who throws at the other team's hitters, you can be sure that some of my hitters are going to be thrown at. It's about the only known cure for the problem.

You hear some people say, "It's part of the game." I've never believed that. Baseball is a game of skill, and deliberate injury has no part in it. For what it might be worth, I don't think that it has a place in any game, except boxing. If you're going out on a field to hurt someone, you can't really say you're playing a game.

On the other hand, I do feel that there is a place in the game for a pitch that makes the batter get out of the way. Let's look at the situation from the pitcher's point of view. He stands sixty feet and six inches away from the plate. That plate is only seventeen inches wide. Unless he throws the ball over the plate, he's doing the batter a favor.

Now, a hitter comes up who stands close to the plate, and leans over it. The pitcher's working area, which is small to begin with, is now made smaller. He has to do something. Asking the batter to move back isn't going to work. So he pitches close to the batter. Maybe it's close enough to move the batter back. I'm for that.

Or let's suppose that the first two pitches are curve balls out away from the batter, and they're both strikes. Now the batter is leaning in that direction. The pitcher can't come back with another one until he straightens that batter up. I'm for that, too.

It's the old theory of "How close can I come to an object without hitting it?" If I hit the batter, he's awarded first base. In the personal battle between the pitcher and the batter, the pitcher has lost. Such defeats can be very costly.

In the chapter on Little League baseball, I'll be talking about the knockdown pitch at that level. But for now, let me say one thing. Any pitcher who depends on it, or uses it a great deal, is a bad pitcher, and one without much future.

The only time it's worthwhile is when it's used for retribution. When a pitcher is knocking down your hitters, you'd better be prepared to knock down some of his. As I said, it's the only way to stop the thing.

I remember one day when we were playing the Phillies, and Robin Roberts was pitching against us. He hit me in the ribs, which was very unusual, because Roberts had good control most of the time. Our pitcher was my roomie, Don Drysdale.

The next time Roberts came up, Drysdale hit him on his backside with a fast ball. Robbie came down to first base. As he and I stood together at the bag, Drysdale was on the mound just glaring at Roberts. Nothing happened for about fifteen seconds. Drysdale stood there glaring, and Roberts was standing with his hands on his knees, looking at the ground. He never looked at Don, but finally he sort of half turned toward me, and I could see he was grinning. He said, very softly, "Tell your roomie I got the message."

Mentioning Roberts brings up another point that all pitchers, and men who handle pitchers, should keep in mind. Baseball is peculiar in that the clock isn't a factor. As long as you're playing, you have a chance to win. A quarterback can look at the clock, and know that the game is already won. Basketball players can do the same thing. But a pitcher must never anticipate that the game is won. It's not a rare thing to see pitchers who relax too early. A lot of pitchers are taken out of games in the late innings, not because they're tired, but because they've anticipated a victory before they got it.

Roberts was unusual in this regard. If Robbie was winning, say, 4 to 0, he wasn't too tough to hit against. He'd give you a ball you could handle. He just went along on the theory that the odds were always in his favor, and that if you hit it, somebody would catch it. Then maybe you'd score a couple of runs. It was

Celebrating the Dodgers' 6 to 3 victory over the Yankees in the first game of the 1956 World Series are Jackie Robinson, who homered in the second inning; winning pitcher Sal Maglie, who struck out ten; and Gil Hodges, who homered, with two on base, in the third inning.

altogether different up at that plate now. Somehow his fast ball was a little faster, and pitches that were coming right down the middle suddenly stayed on the corners.

If the Phillies got him a couple more runs, he'd be nice to hit at again. He could turn it on and off when he wanted to. But there are very few Robin Robertses in this world.

Sal Maglie was the exact opposite. Maglie had to bear down from the first pitch to the last. If he got way ahead, he knew that he couldn't relax and give you good pitches to hit, because when he wanted to go back to being extra sharp, he couldn't do it. Maglie once took an 11 to 0 lead into the fifth inning against the Cardinals. He eased up; the Cardinals got seven runs before Durocher could get Maglie out of there, and the Giants wound up losing, 14 to 12.

Maglie also pointed up another thing about pitching. Preparation. For some reason, Sal had to set up his rhythm of pitching. The word around the league was "If you're going to get to Maglie, you have to do it early." In other words, you'd better hope that you'd get some runs in the first few innings, hopefully enough to knock him out of the box. Every inning he pitched, your chances got slimmer.

I had a pitcher like that on the Mets last year, Tom Seaver. He's an outstanding young pitcher, with an excellent idea of what he has to do on the mound. But I worried about his ability to get the side out in the first couple of innings. If he did that, I figured I was in pretty good shape.

The last point that I want to make about pitching is the most important, I feel. When pitching is discussed, I hear some people say that the most important thing is for the pitcher to be able to throw hard. Other people say it's control. I don't feel that it's either one.

To me, the most important thing that a pitcher can learn, *must* learn, is that once he turns that ball loose, he's an infielder. He's not supposed to watch what happens; he's supposed to be ready to move off that mound and prevent things from happening.

I've heard all the lines that pitchers use to keep from running in the outfield for exercise, including the one about "If running made you a good pitcher, Jesse Owens would be a twenty-game winner." But running strengthens the legs, which are important in the pitcher's delivery, and, even more, it keeps him in shape so that he can do the fielding job that's required of him.

Any time a ball is hit on which the first baseman might have a play, the pitcher should be breaking to cover first base. He might make the trip ten times without getting to field the throw, but there's always that other time. The first baseman moves over, picks up the ball, gets ready to flip to the pitcher, who should be covering, and there's nobody there. There is no way in the world that a manager can excuse that.

If a pitcher gives up an extra base hit, he shouldn't stand around on the mound and say to himself, "Gee, I got a bad break on that one." His job is to back up third base. Don't wait to see if the runner is going to try for third, because by the time you find that out, it might be too late. Get there in time to line yourself up with the throw.

If it looks like the catcher is going to have to take a throw to the plate, make sure you're backing him up. Chances are that he's going to get only one grab to catch that ball and put it on the runner. He doesn't need another spectator; he needs somebody backing him up. And it's the pitcher's job.

Good defensive play is very important to pitchers, yet how many of them do you see practice it once the season starts. Harry Brecheen and Bobby Shantz, just to name two, were good pitchers. Their ability to help themselves defensively enabled them to have a touch of greatness.

Pitching is hard work. It calls for strategy, control (of yourself and the ball), and defensive play. One reason a pitcher doesn't get to play every day is that so much is asked of him when he does play. Only if he's prepared to give all that is asked of him can he hope to earn the most complimentary description he can ask for—to be called "a winning pitcher."

HITTING

"Hitting a baseball is the single most difficult thing to do in sport."

—TED WILLIAMS

IF TED FEELS it's difficult, think how the rest of us must feel. It *is* difficult, and if current batting averages are any indication, it's getting more difficult all the time. But, like all the challenges that athletes face in their favorite sports, it can be tremendously satisfying or tremendously frustrating, depending on what happens.

Hitting a baseball is difficult for a lot of reasons. For one thing, the ball is moving when you swing at it. Not only that; it doesn't follow a straight course from the pitcher's hand to the point where you swing.

Add to that the fact that you're trying to hit a moving object that's round, with a bat that's also round, and roughly the same size in circumference. What that means is that you must not only make contact; you must make it with the solid part of the bat.

You also have to add the element of physical danger. Batters are aware that the ball might hit them, and that has to be taken into consideration. If you think about it too much, chances are that you'll never hit the ball. But if you forget about it altogether, you're going to wind up getting hurt.

Probably the most important factor in the difficulty of hitting is the pitcher. Sixty feet and six inches away from the batter stands a man whose job it is to see that you don't hit the ball. He is well paid, talented, and has a tremendous edge over the hitter in one respect. He knows what the next pitch is going to be. He also has another pretty strong element in his favor, the law of averages.

Let's imagine that a hitter hits .350. With an average like that last year, he not only would have led the National League; he would have led the American league by 49 points. Yet a batter goes to the plate with the idea of getting a base hit, and a .350 hitter *fails* 65 times out of 100.

Before we put aside the slide rule completely, let's take one more example in mathematics. Fans make jokes about .250 hitters, and bow to .300 hitters. But just what is the difference? At the major-league level, a player who plays every day, or practically every day, goes to bat about 600 times a year. At that rate, a .300 hitter will get 180 hits, and a .250 hitter will get 150 hits. That's a difference of 30 hits, or practically one hit a week.

For the secret of how to be a good hitter, I refer you to Ted Williams. He's written some very interesting articles on hitting. Most of the things he points out are things I happen to agree with. There are a few, I feel, that don't apply to most hitters, but only to the ones that are exceptionally gifted, as Williams was.

What I'd like to talk about is hitting, and hitters, as a manager sees it. A manager has to make a determination on who is a good hitter, with only a certain consideration given to a batting average. There are other things that a manager has to consider, and these same things should be considered by the hitters themselves.

There's a cliché that says, "The most underrated play in baseball is a ground ball to the second baseman." Baseball people hear it a lot, and, like most clichés, it's true. No man ever managed a ball club that didn't find himself praying for a ground ball to the second baseman. Also, every manager knows the feeling of not getting it when he wants it.

Here's the situation. The first man up in the inning hits a double. Right here you start looking for that ground ball to the second baseman. If you get it, your runner moves over to third. Then you have a man on third, with one out. With a man on third, there are a lot of ways you can score a run. He can score on a fly ball, on a passed ball, on an error. From second, you need a base hit to score him.

If the batter should hit a ground ball to the shortstop or the third baseman, chances are the runner will be held at second. That's why a ground ball to the second baseman is such an attractive play to a manager.

The batter is asked to give himself up. Instead of trying for a base hit that's going to make his average look better, he's asked to do something that will hurt his batting average but help his ball club. Some hitters can do it; others can't. Some will try; others won't. A player who wants to help his team should learn to do it, and should also be ready to do it.

Personally, I'd like to see the day when the Rules Committee recognizes that a batter who does it is sacrificing himself, the same as a man who bunts with a runner on first. The man who bunts is credited with a sacrifice, and not charged with a time at bat, because he moved the runner from first to second. But the man who hits a ground ball to the second baseman is given no credit, even though he moved a runner from second to third.

The basic thing that a batter must concentrate on is *contact*. Above everything else, he must put the bat on the ball. Once that happens, a lot of things are possible. Without it, nothing can happen.

The late Fresco Thompson, former general manager of the Los Angeles Dodgers, used to tell a story about a try-out camp he was running years ago. A youngster told Fresco that he had a problem, that he was swinging underneath the ball. Fresco asked the boy how far underneath it he was swinging, and the boy said, "About this far," and showed his thumb and index finger about an eighth of an inch apart. Fresco said, "Get yourself some innersoles."

The important thing in hitting is contact, so it might be a good idea here to go back to the basic idea of making that contact.

I've heard a lot of batting instructors over the years tell young players, "The most important thing is to be comfortable at the plate." It's a theory that I don't happen to agree with. If a player is comfortable and doesn't make contact with the ball, he's not going to play. Also, if he hits consistently, he's going to be comfortable.

If comfort was the only thing to take into consideration, just about every hitter would stand the same way. He'd stand with both feet reasonably close together, and the bat would rest on his shoulder. It's just not that simple. The first thing a hitter should do is find a position in which he can consistently make contact with the ball, *then* concentrate on refining that position to its most comfortable stage.

After contact, I would have to say that the next most important thing for a hitter to learn is adjustment. To appreciate better what I mean by "adjustment," let me give you a couple of examples of different kinds of pitchers.

There's an old story about the guy who went up to hit against the great Walter Johnson in the days when Johnson could really fire the ball. It was getting dark, and Johnson was tough to see with the sun shining brightly. Anyway, the umpire called a third strike out on this batter, who started for the dugout, and, over his shoulder, said to the umpire, "It didn't *sound* like a strike to me."

Then take Joe Garagiola's description of hitting against Stu Miller. Joe said that when he hit against Miller he would start to psych himself when he left the bench. He'd keep repeating, "I won't swing too soon. I won't swing too soon." Then, Joe says: "He'd wind up, and show me the glove, the kneecap, the finger-nails, and finally, the ball. I'd keep telling myself, over and over, that I wouldn't swing too soon. Finally, I'd swing, miss, and say to myself, 'Dummy, you swung too soon.' "

Now, it stands to reason that a hitter can't swing the same way against a Walter Johnson and a Stu Miller. They're different kinds of pitchers, and to have any success at all a hitter has to learn to adjust. If the batter swings the same way against all pitchers, then some pitchers are going to chew him up.

It's the same thing with two strikes on a batter. Hitters come to the plate with different ideas of what they want to do. A right-handed hitter might decide that he wants to "take him the other way," that is, to hit the ball to right field. Another might be look-ing for a particular spot to hit the ball, where the defense has left a hole. Some might be thinking they'd like to find out how far they can hit the ball.

But once they have two strikes on them, it's time to adjust and concentrate on making contact. This might mean changing the position of the feet or the grip on the bat. But, once he has two strikes on him, the game has become very simple for the batter. His only job is to make contact.

You hear a lot in baseball about "guess hitters." Ask most ballplayers if they guess on what the pitcher is going to throw them, and they'll tell you that they don't. Strictly speaking, that's just not true.

To a ballplayer, his salary is determined by what he does with the bat in his hand. Every time he goes to the plate, he's waging a very personal war. It's only natural that he tries to anticipate the enemy, especially if the pitcher is giving him a rough time. The longer the rough time continues, the more the batter tries to guess what the pitcher is going to throw. Guessing wrong is the greatest single cause of slumps.

But even good hitters will admit that there is one "guess" that they feel they have to take. They must always look for the fast ball, and adjust to the curve. If they look for the curve, they can't adjust for the fast ball. By the time they try that, the ball is by them.

Another common failing among hitters, especially young ones, is their desire to hit what they call "my" pitch. For example, a hitter likes the ball up, and out over the plate. He hits it better than he hits other ones, so he waits for it. Do you have any idea of how quickly pitchers can figure out what kind of pitch a batter can handle best? Not very long. Once they know, they make it their business to keep the ball away from that area.

I think a manager should tell a hitter to look for a ball that he can handle, that is, one that he can make solid contact with. Don't look for one that he can hit over the fence, because he's going to get calluses waiting for it. Also, he must learn to handle everything that's in the strike zone. If he doesn't, he's giving the pitcher another edge.

Knowing the strike zone, naturally, is an important part of any hitter's job. Some hitters never learn it. I honestly feel that a hitter is not always a good judge of whether or not a ball is in the strike zone. I think one reason that I didn't complain very often about called strikes is the fact that I broke in as a catcher. I had a chance to hear a lot of hitters complain about pitches that I could see were good ones.

Catchers, incidentally, are inclined to use one line on umpires that the men in blue don't like very much. I've heard it a lot. I remember one day when I was batting, and the umpire, Beans Reardon, called the pitch a ball. The catcher said, "Beansie, why is it that when I'm hitting, that pitch is a strike, but when I'm catching it's a ball?" Through his mask, I could hear Beansie's high-pitched voice saying, "If you want to hit again today,

Gil Hodges, in his den at home, gazes at the picture of baseball immortal
Babe Ruth.

Buster, you'd better stop asking those smart questions."

At whatever level, the biggest job that a manager can do for a hitter is to try to show the player just what kind of hitter he is. Some players are power hitters; others aren't. A manager has to make a determination as to whether he wants a player to hit with power or hit for an average.

It's true that some players can do both: a Stan Musial, a Willie Mays, a Mickey Mantle, a Hank Aaron. But they're superstars, and what makes them superstars is the fact that they can hit with power, and do it for an average.

When you look at the record of a Babe Ruth, you get an idea of why he's still remembered today, and always will be. Ruth hit 714 home runs. He had a lifetime batting average of .342.

Let's examine that. Coming into the 1969 season, Willie Mays is second to Ruth in the all-time home-run list. Willie will be thirty-eight years old shortly after the season starts. If he plays four more years, and averages 30 home runs a year, he still won't catch Ruth. As a further point, last year Willie hit 23 home runs.

In the matter of batting average, let's compare Ruth with the man generally regarded to be the greatest batter of all time, Ty Cobb. Cobb was a different kind of hitter. His long suit wasn't power. He's the only man ever to get more than 4,000 base hits. Yet, although he got about 1,300 more hits than Ruth did, Ruth hit six times as many home runs as Cobb. What I'm trying to say is that there is a place for both kinds of hitters, but to expect to find them both in the same man is a very rare thing.

When a manager decides that he's going to go along with a player as a power hitter, he must make up his mind to live with strikeouts. To hit with power, a batter must swing hard. If he swings hard, he's going to strike out a lot. It's up to the manager to decide whether or not he can live with that luxury. Some can; some can't. A lot depends on the kind of team he has.

Let me give you an example that I'm very familiar with. Gil

Hodges. When I retired, I'd hit 370 major-league home runs. I suppose that I shouldn't mention that, but I'd be silly to say that I'm not proud of it. At that time, no National League right-handed hitter had hit more. But, much as I like to talk about it, that's not really what I'm trying to prove.

What I *am* trying to prove is something that I don't particularly enjoy talking about. I struck out over 1,100 times. Now, that's a lot of walking back to the dugout. Yet the managers that I played for, without exception, went along with me. Some of them tried to help me to cut down on my strikeouts, but not at the expense of changing my way of hitting. Looking back now, I can see their reasons for it.

In the first place, they could afford it with the kind of club that we had. We had good hitters in Brooklyn, and there was always a good chance of one guy picking up the others. Also, we played in a small ball park, so home runs weren't hard to come by for either team. If we gave up two or three runs with one swing of the bat, we had to be able to get them back the same way.

I don't honestly know how Gil Hodges, the manager, would handle Gil Hodges, the player. When I was playing, there were some nice parks to hit in, but that's changing all the time. The last World Series was a good example. The St. Louis park is tough on hitters, especially power hitters. You can hit the ball hard four times in that park, and wind up without a hit. It happens all the time.

Detroit, on the other hand, is a great park to hit in. Detroit is an old ball park, and I think, generally, that you'll find that old parks were built for hitters, and the newer ones are being built more for pitchers. The point is that a manager doesn't mind swapping strikeouts for the home runs he knows will come, but in today's parks he has a lot less chance of getting those home runs.

Pitchers have a greater "giveaway" area in these parks than they used to have. By that I mean that they'll let you hit the ball more because there's less chance of you hitting it out of the park. I'm talking about power hitters now. A good example is the story told by Monte Irvin, once a fine hitter with the Giants, and then an assistant to Baseball Commissioner William Eckert. Irvin was a strong hitter. He tells about a day in the Polo Grounds when he batted against Warren Spahn. For those of you who don't remember the Polo Grounds, the two foul lines were very short, but center field was 481 feet deep.

Anyway, Irvin says he hit four balls off Spahn really hard. Each one went over 420 feet. But at the end of the day, Monte didn't have a base hit to show for his efforts. Spahn had given him pitches to hit, but they were all out away from Irvin, so that he couldn't pull them down the line.

Which brings up another thing that managers must do for a hitter. Hitters will really cream a ball, say 400 feet to dead center, and then see it get caught. They come back to the bench and talk about how lucky the pitcher was, because the ball had been hit so well. It's the manager's job to point out to the hitter —but not right then—that the batter had done exactly what the pitcher wanted him to do. The ball was hit hard, but it was the pitcher who chose the direction in which it was hit. All good pitchers do that.

Now, let's get away from the power hitters for a while, and concentrate on the other kinds of batters. One is the "singles" hitter, like Matty Alou or Pete Rose. They concentrate on base hits, and they have both been very successful. I can't help feeling that we are going to see more and more of that kind of hitter as the ball parks get bigger. It's not that the home run will ever become unpopular, only that it's going to be harder to come by.

In addition to helping their batting averages, they also help the power hitters on their team. The batter can always count on getting better pitches to hit when there are men on base. Also, the power hitters are paid to drive in runs, and to do that they need men on base.

Another category altogether is the "hit-and-run" man. Two fine examples would be Dick Groat and Alvin Dark, when they were playing. Their secret is, first, contact, but also bat control. They not only put the bat on the ball, but they direct the ball where it can serve the best possible purpose. A manager who has that kind of hitter can afford to gamble with the hit-and-run, which can be the most important play in baseball.

When you talk about the hit-and-run, the first question is whether it's an offensive or a defensive play. There are two schools of thought on that subject. The ones who say it's a defensive play hold that the primary reason for using it is to stay out of the double play. Others feel that its basic purpose is to move a runner from first to third on a single that might ordinarily keep him at second. For what it's worth, I think it's an offensive play, but I see the merit of the other side of it, too.

I've seen a lot of good hit-and-run batters, but I single out Dark and Groat because I think they might have been the best that I ever played against. Billy Herman was another who's considered outstanding, but I didn't see that much of Billy as a player. But Groat and Dark could do it all. When they were ready to play hit-and-run, it was almost impossible to stop them. Since they were both right-handed hitters, they both worked much the same way. The runner would break with the pitch, and they would generally hit the ball to right field. Since the second baseman figured to move over to cover the bag, there was a big hole in the infield, and that's where they would hit.

Logically, it would seem that the way to stop it would be to throw the ball inside to them. Yet both of them have told me that they would rather play hit-and-run with an inside pitch than with one that was away from them. They had two reasons. First, the ball was easier to handle if it was in close. Second, if they saw the shortstop break instead of the second baseman, they could hit the ball to the left-field side. Now you see what I mean by bat control.

The hit-and-run play eventually became a problem between Groat and one of his managers. It was while Dick was playing for the St. Louis Cardinals, and the manager was the late Johnny Keane. The club was going badly, and Johnny felt that some steps should be taken. One of them was that he would no longer let Groat put on the hit-and-run play himself. Until then, when Groat felt that the hit-and-run was called for, and that he could handle the pitcher well enough, he would have his own sign with the runner on first that the play was on. But Keane stopped that.

Well, nobody asked me, but I've got an opinion anyway, and since we're talking about managing, I'd like to have my say. For me, the manager, and only the manager, should put on the hit-and-run. No matter how good the hitter, there is a danger involved. It's the manager's job to determine the strategy for the entire ball club, and the best way to do that is to make the decisions yourself. If the play backfires, it can cost you a ball game, and the manager has to take the blame. If he's going to take the blame, he might as well take it for something he thought of himself.

The other dangerous offensive play is the "squeeze." The squeeze play is a great play to watch, and it calls for a combination of things. The batter must make contact; the runner must have speed; and the manager has to have a little guts. There are very few occasions when he has a chance to look as good—or as bad. It also helps considerably if the other team doesn't know that the play is on.

If it's properly worked, the squeeze play is an exciting thing. The runner breaks down the line from third—and doesn't stop. Now everyone knows the play is on, and the only question is whether or not it's too late. The batter is under pressure because he knows that he must make contact when he bunts, or the whole thing will backfire. The catcher is trying to watch the ball and the runner at the same time. The pitcher is, hopefully, charging the plate, and the whole crowd is on its feet.

When it works it's beautiful. It's just that so many things can go wrong. The batter squares away to bunt too soon, and the pitcher throws the ball where it can't be bunted. Or the runner slips coming down the base line. Or the catcher picks up your sign, and there's a pitchout. Or the batter misses the ball. Or somebody misses the sign. Of course, if you get really unlucky, the batter will hit a little foul ball, and the whole thing can turn into a double play against you.

Starting that runner from third is always dangerous. I remember Charlie Dressen telling me about an incident when he was managing the Washington club. Charley had a Cuban on the club who never took a lead off third base. Since the Cuban had problems with English, and Dressen spoke no Spanish, Charley tried to give him the message in sign language that he should move off the base when the pitcher delivered the ball. But he just couldn't get through.

Finally, Charley went to another Cuban, Julio Becquer, and got him to act as interpreter. Becquer's English was good, and Charley had him tell his countryman that he had to move off third base when the ball was delivered. They even worked out a key word that Charley could use as a reminder.

Well, the next time the Cuban got to third base, Charley was coaching there. He gave his man the word signal, and sure enough the runner moved with the pitch. But after he got about ten feet off the bag, he just stood there. The catcher started to throw the ball back to the pitcher, spotted the runner, and picked him off. Charley would laugh and say, "I taught him all about gettin' off the bag, but I forgot to tell him about comin' back."

In any discussion of hitters, you must get around eventually to pitchers as hitters. Pitchers are notoriously weak hitters, although there are certainly some exceptions. But for the most part, they're bad hitters. Below the professional level, pitchers get more opportunity to take batting practice. At the professional level, especially in the major leagues, they don't get enough batting practice, and I'm all for something being done about it.

After all, a pitcher, especially if he's going well and you want to keep him in the game, is one-ninth of your offense. Pitchers who complain about not being allowed to finish a tight ball game might help their cause by working more on their hitting. I had a pitcher come to me last year to ask for extra batting practice. I told him I'd be glad to arrange it when the team was at home, providing the pitchers would report to the park early for the extra practice. I never heard any more about the subject.

We had a pitcher last year named Jerry Koosman, who won nineteen games and who looks like one of baseball's brightest young stars. I was leaning on the batting cage one day, watching Koosman take batting practice, and I finally said to him, "With a swing like that, if you ever get a hit, I'll buy you a bottle of champagne." In Atlanta, I wound up going for, not one, but two bottles of champagne, because Koosman not only got a base hit; he drove in a run with it. Koosman and the little old wine maker both had a big day.

There are very few things that a manager can do for a hitter once he steps into the batter's box. One of the great things about baseball is the fact that, despite the importance of teamwork, there comes a time when a batter is strictly on his own. In the instant between the time that the ball leaves the pitcher's hand and it arrives at the plate, there's not much time for anything but reflex actions.

However, managers can advise hitters on certain little things that might come in handy. For example, a hitter would be wise to take an instant between pitches to check the defense. On a well-organized team, the infielders know what the catcher is calling for. They might move accordingly. If they do, the batter should get an idea (*a*) what the pitch might be, and (*b*) where there is apt to be a hole he can hit the ball through.

Another tip is one that Roger Maris used to use. To make sure that he didn't get into the habit of overstriding, which can be very bad for a hitter, Maris used to smooth out the dirt in the batter's box after each pitch. When the ball was delivered, Maris would stride. Then he would check the spike marks in the dirt to see if he was striding too far. After checking, he'd smooth out the dirt again before the next pitch.

The swing of the bat is not a constant thing. Even the great hitters would occasionally get out of their "groove." A grooved swing, especially to a power hitter, is the key to the good year. It's a swing that starts early enough to pull the ball, and has enough of an arc to get underneath the ball and give it the lift that it needs. Maris, incidentally, in 1961 had the classic "grooved" swing. If you ever get an opportunity to see movies of Roger on his way to setting the new home-run record that year, pay particular attention to the swing. You can tell the ball is gone almost at the moment of contact.

In discussing hitting, you hear the phrase "clutch hitter" used a lot. It's an abused phrase. Some hitters seem to react better than others in tight situations, but I think if you research it you'd find that it's because they find themselves in more tight situations. There are a great many factors involved, such as the ability of teammates to get on base ahead of you, the men who might be hitting behind you, and every ballplayer's best girl, Lady Luck.

For example, John Smith comes to bat with two men on, two out in the ninth inning, and his team trailing by one run. He hits a hard line drive; the third baseman makes a leaping catch; and the game is over. The next day, in the same situation, he gets fooled completely on a pitch, swings late, hits the ball on the end of the bat; it falls behind the first baseman, and two runs score. John Smith is now a "clutch" hitter.

Hitting is a physical act, but it's also a mental one. Let's go back to something I mentioned earlier—fear. The batter must use his brain to conquer that fear, which, like all other fears, doesn't stand up too well against logic. Let's suppose that he's knocked down with the first pitch. Immediately, he should start to think. The first question, of course, is "Did he do it on purpose?" If the situation of the game rules that out, then it can be dismissed. If, however, there's the chance that it was done on purpose, then the hitter must realize that he's now one pitch ahead. He must use whatever psychological method he prefers to drive that last pitch out of his mind. I'm not saying that's easy. Just that it's necessary.

It's the same way if the first pitch is a called strike, which the batter thought was a ball. Forget it. That pitch is over and done with. It's no longer important. The next one is the important one. Sometimes an angry hitter is a better hitter, but not usually. A hitter who concentrates on the last pitch instead of the next one is doing the pitcher a favor, and hitters aren't up there to do pitchers favors.

One of my favorite stories on that subject is one that Gus Mauch tells. It concerns a guy who was an outstanding hitter for years in the Pacific Coast League, Joe Brovia. Gus was playing with the old Los Angeles club in the Coast League, and one of the pitchers was an old teammate of mine, Eddie Chandler. Brovia had been wearing Chandler out all season.

This day, Brovia came up to hit, and the first pitch put him right on the seat of his pants. On the bench, his teammates started hollering, "Go out there and punch him, Joe. Don't take that." But Brovia never looked at them. The next pitch was in the same place, and the cries from the bench got louder. "Don't let him do that, Joe. Go out there and flatten him." At this, Brovia turned toward his bench and said, almost pathetically, "I would, but he's too good to hit at."

In talking about hitters, there are three names I feel that I have to mention. One is Stan Musial. There's no doubt in my mind that Musial is the best hitter I ever saw. I take nothing away from Ted Williams, because the record tells you what he could do. But I played against him in only a few spring training games and a couple of All-Star games. Musial I saw a lot more of. Too much, to be honest.

I don't pick Musial because of his record. I only have to close my eyes to remember the kind of hitter he was. He could hit for an average, of course. He could also hit with power. Many people overlook Stan's power, because he never led the league in home runs. Not once in his long career. Yet he hit 475 of them in his lifetime.

Stan could hit to all fields, and hit the ball hard, too. He was also a good team hitter. By that I mean that he could play hit-and-run, although he wasn't asked to too much. I remember that in the 1949 All-Star game, which was played in Ebbets Field, Musial gave an excellent example of what kind of hitter he was. Maybe I should point out first that in All-Star games, there is very little use of strategy. Everyone is pretty much on his own.

In the third inning, Jackie Robinson led off with a walk. Musial was the next hitter, and Virgil Trucks, a guy with a great fast ball, was pitching. Robinson decided to steal. As Robinson broke, shortstop Eddie Joast broke for second. Just that quickly, Musial shifted his feet, and singled through the hole made by Joast's break. In the box score the next day it looked like just another base hit for Musial, but it was a perfect offensive play.

Robinson is another player that I have to mention, because he is probably the most complete offensive player that I can remember. He could bunt; he could hit with power. He helped other hitters on his club when he was on base because he was a distraction to the pitcher. Whether he was on first base or on third, he was a constant threat to steal. And add to all those things the fact that he was as good as any I've ever seen at protecting the plate with two strikes on him (that is, that he got at least a piece of any pitch that could possibly be a strike). The best way I can sum him up is to say that he was exciting to watch from the stands, and just as exciting to watch from the bench.

The third hitter I would like to mention is Roy Campanella.

We hear a lot now about Campy, and the fact that he's an inspiration to a lot of youngsters. To my way of thinking, Campy was an inspiration to a lot of kids even when he was playing. First of all, if your memories of Roy Campanella are only of him in a wheelchair, I'd like to point out one thing that should tell you what kind of player he was. In nine full years in the major leagues, Campy was the National League's Most Valuable Player three times. Nuf said.

Now, in his playing days, Campy had a problem. Sidearm right-handed pitching was tough on Campy. Very tough. Yet he made himself an outstanding hitter rather than let that run him out of baseball. His problem was added to by the fact that the Dodgers saw right-handers almost exclusively in those days. We had a good hitting ball club, but Campy, Pee Wee Reese, Carl Furillo, Robinson, Billy Cox, and I were all right-handed. So was Andy Pafko, who was our left fielder for a while. As a result, we didn't see many left-handers.

Now, none of us liked that good sidearm right-hander, but Campy could be made to look worse than most players. But that pitcher had better not make a mistake. Campy "hung tough" (had the courage to stick it out in a tough situation) and got the job done. Maybe that's why none of us who were his teammates were surprised at the way he "hung tough" after his accident.

The job of helping a hitter is one of the toughest a manager faces. Yet it's part of the job, and that goes for whatever kind of team he's managing. I'd like to close out with some tips, not for hitters, but for the men who manage hitters. Every hitter has different problems, and the solutions are up to the manager and the hitter. But I should like to point out some things that hold in almost all cases.

1. CONTACT. Everything must start there. Bring him to that point before you start on such things as power or placing the ball.

2. SUGGEST. You can't order a player to hit a certain way. Also, there is more than one way to hit. There's no one style that's the only way. Suggest that he try one thing, then another. It's important for a manager to remember that everybody doesn't hit the same way he did.

3. WORK. If you suggest something, and it works, don't walk away. Watch, encourage, and remember that one hard-hit ball isn't necessarily the sign that the problem is solved.

4. AVOID. Don't mess with a successful hitter. I don't care if he's standing on his head, if he's hitting the ball, leave him alone. Also, once you get him out of a slump, don't keep after him. You're apt to coach him right back into another one.

5. REMEMBER. If you've got a hitter who's breaking your heart because he's going badly, remember the quote from Ted Williams at the begining of this chapter: "Hitting a baseball is the single most difficult thing to do in sport." He's right.

DEFENSE

DEFENSE IS THE LEAST sensational part of baseball, and, because of that, I feel that it's the least appreciated. In that sense, I'm talking about the feelings of those who are not directly involved in baseball as a livelihood. Pitching is more glamorous; hitting is more exciting; but defense is the key to a sound and solid baseball team.

In discussing defense, there are several points that should be kept in mind:

1. A team can win even if the pitcher doesn't strike out a single batter. It's even possible, although unlikely, that a team can win without getting a base hit. But in any nine-inning game, twenty-seven batters *have* to be retired on the losing team.
2. Of the various things that make up a baseball team, such as pitching, hitting, power, speed, and defense, one can be taught more easily than the rest, and that's defense.

3. There is no way the opposition can offset a good defense. As an example, a good hitter can be walked in a certain situation in order to protect against his offensive ability. But there's no way to protect against a player's defensive ability.

4. While it's true that an overpowering pitcher can dominate a game, it's also true that such pitchers are rare, and even if a big-league club does have such a pitcher, he can work only once every four or five days. The defense is there every day, and unless it's a good one, it can seriously curtail the effectiveness of any pitcher, no matter how strong.

The simplest way I know to explain my estimation of the importance of defense is to say this: The good defensive club gets beaten. The bad defensive club beats itself.

Let's examine the postwar record of the New York Yankees. When you hear about the Yankees, the immediate thought is of their power. Yet the thing that impressed me most about the Yankees was the fact that they rarely beat themselves. The importance of that might be shown this way. From 1949 through 1964, the Yankees won the American League pennant in each year but two. In how many of those years do you think a Yankee batter led the American League in home runs? The answer is five.

Remember now, this is a team that won fourteen pennants in sixteen years. How many of those years do you think the Yankees led the league in home runs as a team? It's five again, plus one tie. If you still think that the Yankees' success was due to hitting alone, here's another question. How many of those sixteen years did the Yankees lead the league in team batting average? The answer is six, and in one of those six years they didn't win the pennant.

It's obvious that defense played a tremendous role. You can't overlook their pitching, it's true. But when you rate the effectiveness of a pitcher, you must consider his earned-run average, and I believe that defense is a factor in that figure. Certainly, there are outstanding pitchers, the ones I mentioned before who dominate a game. Yet in the fourteen years that the Yankees won pennants over that stretch, they did it six times without a twenty-game winner on their staff.

I'm using these figures as an illustration that defense had to play a tremendous part in their success. Maybe I should point out here that I'm not bringing fielding averages into this because I don't honestly feel that they are a good yardstick. They don't recognize the value of a fielder who makes errors because he tries, and they reward the fielder who doesn't try to handle the difficult play. Also, there is no allowance for the mental error, which will beat you just as often as the physical error.

Now, I'm not trying to give the impression that the Yankees of that era were players who never made an error. Of course they did. But they cut their mental errors down to a minimum. In run-down plays, the ball was handled as few times as possible. (The more times it's handled, the greater the opportunity for it to be dropped or for another runner to advance.) The throws from the outfield were designed to hit the cutoff man, so that if a runner couldn't be stopped from scoring, at least another runner couldn't move into scoring position.

The thing about defense, as far as youngsters are concerned, is that plain hard work can make a boy a better defensive player. Hard work can't make a slow boy run faster, change a weak throwing arm into a strong one, or give a pitcher a fast ball that he never had before. But, defensively, a player can be improved by hard work, even changed from a bad one to a good one.

As I mentioned earlier, it's tough for me to remember a short-stop who didn't have a stronger arm than Phil Rizzuto. It's also tough to remember a better shortstop than he was. The difference was hard work. He taught himself to get rid of the ball quickly, and that, along with good hands, made him an outstanding infielder.

In the National League, Dick Groat came to the Pittsburgh

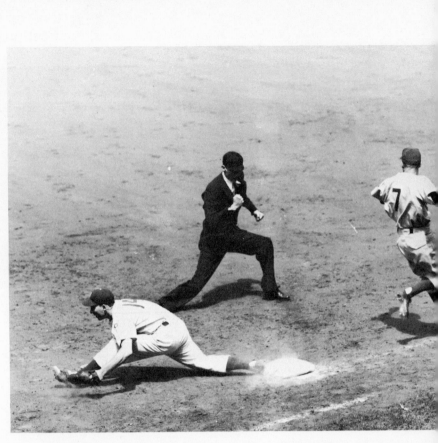

The long stretch that can get a batter out in a close play.

Triple play. In the third inning of the Dodgers–Boston Braves game on April 26, 1949, at Ebbets Field, Gene Hermanski grabbed a short fly hit by Alvin Dark to right field. He fired to Jackie Robinson to get Johnny Sain, who had been on second base, and then Robinson threw to Hodges to get Ed Stanky, who had been on first.

club without great ability as a shortstop, but made himself into an outstanding one. Groat became a master at what infielders call "cheating." That doesn't mean he broke any rules. What he did was to anticipate, by knowing the batter and what the pitcher was going to throw to him, where the ball was likely to be hit. Then he'd take an extra step or two in that direction. As a result, he threw out a lot of batters who otherwise would have got base hits.

There are tricks like that for every position, but, like any other little trick in any business, the real art comes in knowing how and when to perform it. Also, tricks alone are never the answer. There are certain basics that should be remembered.

Baseball presents problems different from those in other games in the area of defense. For one thing, there is much more emphasis on reaction. A baseball team can't depend on one man to stop one other man, as in basketball or football. Also, because baseball defense often calls for more than one man to be involved, teamwork among defensive players becomes more important.

In football or basketball, the key defensive play usually involves the area on the playing field where the ballcarrier or intended pass receiver, or shooter or passer, happens to be. In baseball, a center fielder picks up a ball four hundred feet from home plate, fires it to a relay man who, in turn, throws it to a catcher to make a tag. The defense hasn't done its job until that tag is made, and unless the ball is handled rapidly and cleanly by everyone involved, chances are that the defensive play won't succeed.

There is one basic thing that a player must learn to become a good defensive baseball player. Before each pitch, he must say to himself, "What am I going to do with the ball after I catch it?" Some players substitute the word "if" for "after." I don't think that *they* can ever really be good defensive players.

Another important thing for *all* defensive players—and this includes pitchers and catchers—is that while they are on the field they should forget a phrase that's usually sound advice, "Be seen but not heard." The player who's fielding the ball is forced to keep his eye on it, and the others should let him know that they aren't going to run into him. Also, they should advise him what to do with it after he catches it. If the fielder sees that he can make the play, and realizes that he can probably handle it best, he should let the other players know that he's going after it. This is a great help in preventing balls from falling in, accidents from happening, and managers from getting gray.

Defensive skills are usually developed pretty well by the time a player reaches the major leagues. With youngsters, it can be a problem, but a problem where steps can be taken to solve it. I've often thought that if I were managing a team of youngsters, and that includes all nonprofessionals, I might like to try an interesting experiment in teaching defense.

At the professional level, infielders and outfielders and catchers usually take part in a routine practice drill. I'm not opposed to that, by any means. I think every team should do it, because it's a help to a very definite part of defensive play: rhythm.

However, it does have one drawback. Let's say that I'm a third baseman. During that workout, I know exactly when the ball is going to be hit to me, and when it's going to be thrown to me. But when the game starts, I don't have that advance notice. I don't get the opportunity of setting myself, knowing that the next ball will be coming to me. Not only that, but it will be hit with the idea that I can handle it fairly easily.

If I get a chance to work out by fielding balls that I don't expect, it stands to reason that I'm better prepared when the game gets under way. During the game I not only don't get advance notice that the ball will be hit to me, but it often comes at me a great deal harder than it does during infield practice.

The routine infield drill, I repeat, should not be abandoned. It's a good thing for a player's confidence, and confidence is just as important to a fielder as it is to a hitter. I simply feel that there is much to be said for a drill where the ball is hit to a fielder who doesn't know in advance that he's going to have to handle it.

There are a few suggestions that I'd make to managers who are in charge of teams of nonprofessional players, especially youngsters. You get no written guarantee that they'll work, but I honestly feel that they're worth a try.

One of the biggest problems that managers find these days is getting someone to be the catcher. You don't look for any particular necessary characteristics. You just look for volunteers. The biggest reason that kids don't want to catch is that they feel that they can't do it and that they might get hurt doing it. Also, that cliché about "the tools of ignorance" isn't much help, either.

Personally, I feel that for the boy who really loves baseball, no position will give him the satisfaction that he can get from catching. He and the pitcher make the strategy, and he has the edge of playing every day. Plus that, the whole game is out in front of him, so that he can study the constant battle between offense and defense.

I want to pause right here to make a point. If you're managing a team of youngsters, and you're not letting the catcher call the signals, you are depriving the kids of a big part of the game. If he has problems in that area, work with him. If he wants help, give it to him. But don't arbitrarily decide that you're going to be a genius at his expense.

Now, back to making catching a little easier. If you have a boy on your team that you think might become a catcher, try an experiment with him. Get a pitcher on the mound, you in the batter's box, and the would-be catcher in his position. Then tell him that you're going to swing when the ball is thrown, but you're deliberately *not* going to hit it. The idea is for him to see the bat swung in front of his face, and come to realize that he can still catch the ball. After a couple of days, you might notice a change in his attitude toward catching.

Too much of this sort of thing can be bad, because the boy can develop lazy habits that can be harmful. But it might serve a useful purpose in introducing him to catching. After all, the only thing left for him to learn is how to handle foul tips, and I'm afraid there's just no way to practice that.

In any discussion of defense, there is one basic thing that must be taught to every player on the team—get in front of the ball—that is, get your body in line with the ball so that if it gets through your hands, your body will stop it. Now, obviously, that's not always possible, but it's essential to be sure that your players do it whenever they can. I mention this here because it's especially important to catchers.

Every baseball player, no matter how experienced or inexperienced he may be, is going to make errors. Young players should be reminded of this every once in a while, and their managers shouldn't forget it, either. But the damage that results from that error can be cut down by the player who gets his body in front of the ball.

It's just this simple—the ball that bounces off your glove and then hits your body winds up in front of you. But if your body doesn't stop the ball, it goes past you. For a catcher, it's the difference between a runner advancing or holding his base. The same thing, basically, holds for the players at the other positions.

The manager helps himself and the infielders if he emphasizes that their job is not merely to handle the ball that is hit or thrown to them. There are the very simple basics that must be learned, but there is always another step that you can give them after they have learned one phase.

The first baseman and the third baseman learn to protect the foul lines in certain situations. The first baseman learns to hold runners on base, to act as the cutoff man on throws from the outfield, and to be alert for pick-off throws from the pitcher or catcher.

The second baseman and shortstop should be taught to back

each other up at all times. They should also be taught never to leave the base unprotected. Each should learn to advise the other, depending on which one is fielding the ball, whether or not the double play should be tried. They should work together to decide who is going to cover the bag in any given situation. These are all things that the manager can work on with the players. He is the best judge of what is needed, the proper time, and the boy himself.

The manager's problem in working with a youngster who's going to play third base is probably the most challenging, and potentially rewarding, of that in any field position. In the first place, the third baseman figures to see less defensive action than any other player. Keeping him alert is important, because if he has a tendency to daydream, other teams are going to take advantage of it. He has to exert himself to be sure that the opposition knows that he's there and that he's ready. Sustaining the interest of a youngster who goes inning after inning without fielding the ball is a test for a manager.

When it comes to outfielders, I would recommend to managers of youngsters' teams that they bring their outfielders together for a meeting—not a lecture, now, but a meeting. The first point to make is that the ball is to be thrown into the infield on a low trajectory. As long as the ball isn't over the fielder's head, there's a chance to do something with it. It might be bobbled, but somebody else might back up and protect that bobble from being too costly. But if no one can reach the ball, well, the damage can be tremendous. Make sure that you promise to give the outfielders a chance to practice their throwing. Then keep the promise.

But the most important part of the meeting, I feel, is to let them know that they are dependent on one another for the amount of help they can be to the team and the amount of fun that they'll get out of playing. They must remember one thing: Spectators are not allowed on the playing field. If you're on the field, be ready to play the game.

Outfielders should be taught to back each other up. This helps the team because the damage done by errors is minimized. It helps the players themselves because it allows them to be more aggressive. Let's take a sinking line drive, hit to the left of the center fielder. He may not be sure whether or not he can catch it, but he can certainly give it a better try if he knows that the right fielder is coming over to back him up.

If outfielders are taught to move where the ball is hit, they become better outfielders, and get more out of the game. The younger the boy, the more important this is. Youngsters' arms are not going to be as strong, so that another outfielder might move over to help out with getting the ball into the infield.

The reason I stress the meeting is that if it's made clear to the outfielders that they are operating as a unit, they will have a tendency to make sure that they hustle, if only because they know that the other outfielders are looking for it. It is a hazard of managing, at all levels, that most players are more concerned about looking bad to other players than they are to the manager. Faultfinding is expected from the manager. It hurts much more to find that the other players agree with him.

On the overall defense of youngsters, I hope that managers emphasize all the time that errors are a part of the game and that players shouldn't be too critical of a teammate who makes one. If young players are taught to ask themselves one question before they criticize, your job will be a lot simpler. It's not whether or not a teammate caught the ball, it's "Did he give it a try?" That's very important, because from Little League to the major leagues, that try is the one thing that each player owes to his teammates.

The more a manager works with a youngster on the different phases of defense, the bigger favor he is doing for the boy, the team, and himself. A manager can teach a boy to catch a ball, and to throw it, if not farther, more accurately. As the boy learns these things, baseball becomes more and more enjoyable for him. That enjoyment is a reward that should be worth more than any championship to a manager.

STRATEGY

STRATEGY SOUNDS LIKE a complicated subject, so it might help to keep in mind that the basic essential of baseball strategy—from Little League through the big leagues—is "Keep it simple." The biggest danger for a manager, and the easiest trap for him to fall into, is to overmanage. Baseball, more than most major sports, depends very little on preplanned plays. Because the key thing is reacting to what happens, being a "genius" doesn't really help that much.

I certainly don't mean that you shouldn't make any preparations or that you shouldn't try a play occasionally. I just mean that so much of the game is out of your hands that trying to control it is not only useless but can also be harmful.

Before we talk about what should be avoided, let's go over some of the things that are done. The strategy is supposed to begin with a pregame meeting, so let's look at the two basic kinds of meetings that a manager holds.

First, the offensive meeting. This is for the purpose of giving, or reviewing, the signs that your team will use. Here again the idea is to keep them simple. Anybody can make up a set of signs that the other team will never be able to steal. The trouble with that is that they get so complicated your own players don't get them, either.

Before we get into signs, let's stop for a moment to look at the matter of sign-stealing. We read and hear a lot about one club stealing the signs of another club. The advantages of knowing what the other club has in mind are obvious. But I feel that below the professional level, stealing signs is overrated.

Here's a tip that might help. If the team is on defense, and you wonder about whether or not the batter might be bunting to advance a runner on first, advise your pitcher to throw over to first. On his motion, especially if he's left-handed, the batter may tip him off by squaring away too soon. Now you know that he was bunting, but before you set your defense to guard against the bunt, there's another thing to remember. The sign may now be changed.

Just one further note on the subject of bunting, this time from the offensive side. When you have a man bunting, be sure that he knows *why* he's bunting. If his job is to move a runner along, he should concentrate on doing that, and not so much on reaching first base safely. Unless he makes contact, the play has been useless. Bunting for a base hit is one thing; bunting to move along the runner is something else. That's why they call the second one a sacrifice. While the man who sacrifices is going to try to make first base safely, he has to be prepared to give himself up for the team.

The signs, as I said, should be kept simple. There should be a sign when the hitter is to bunt, another when he's to take a pitch, another when the hit-and-run is on, and another for the base runner to steal. Let's look at each one individually.

A bunt is ordered, primarily, to move a runner along. Occasionally, a manager might notice that a third baseman is playing too deep, and the bunt might very well result in a base hit. In either case, the batter should get as much notice as possible that he is to bunt and why he's to bunt. Bunting is not so easy as it looks, and if you've got a good bunter on your team you'd do well to take advantage of it.

Taking a pitch is done in certain situations. Usually, if a take sign is given, it's done when the batter is ahead of the pitcher. Batters should be looking to see if they're taking or swinging away any time the count is two balls and no strikes, three balls and no strikes, or three balls and one strike. The primary purpose is to test the control of the pitcher, and should he fail that test, set up a base on balls, or a pitch without a lot on it.

The younger the player, the less he should be asked to take. We get back again to it being a game. Taking a pitch is not really all that much fun. He came to the ball park to swing a bat. Let him swing it.

I don't mean that he should *never* take a pitch. Let's say that you're managing, and your team is batting in the last half of the last inning. You've got the bases loaded, and the count on your batter is three balls and no strikes. Have him take a pitch. If it's ball four, the game is over, and you've won. If the pitch is a strike, the count is still your way. This isn't a hard-and-fast rule, just a suggestion.

Taking pitches can become a bad habit. Pee Wee Reese used to go into streaks of taking, whether the pitch was a good one or not. I can remember him saying, "It's funny, but every once in a while I'll find myself kneeling in the on-deck circle, knowing that I'm going to take the first pitch, no matter where it is." That can be bad, because it can put the batter into a hole right away.

Years and years ago, there was an umpire named Bill Byron,

who was known as "The Singing Umpire." One of his little ditties was directed at hitters who took good pitches. Byron would call "Strike," then croon to the batter:

"You'll learn before you get much older,
You can't hit the ball with the bat on your shoulder."

Having taken some good pitches in my time, I really think I could get along without an umpire singing to me about it.

The hit-and-run could cover a book all by itself. The manager has to take the responsibility for it. As far as he's concerned, it's a "guts" play. If anything goes wrong, the manager really should take the blame himself, because there is such a risk of things going badly. (I'm excluding the possibility of the base runner, or the batter, missing the sign. As a manager, I know that can happen, but I don't really blame myself when that happens. My players will tell you that.)

As I've mentioned before, there are mixed feelings about whether the hit-and-run is an offensive or a defensive play. I can remember a discussion I had one night with Joe Garagiola about that. Joe maintained that it was a defensive play, since the primary reason it was used was to stay out of the double play. I felt, and still feel, that it's an offensive play, where the primary idea is to move a runner from first to third so that he can score much more easily. After a long discussion, I think Joe agreed with some of what I said, just as I agreed with some of what he said. But neither of us changed his mind.

Advising managers of kid's teams about using the hit-and-run is tough. Keeping in mind that the idea of the game is having fun, the hit-and-run, when it works, can be very satisfying for a youngster. On the other hand, you put a little pressure on a boy that he might not care for, which could take away from the enjoyment. The best thing I can say is that a manager should know his players, and use his own judgment about who can, and who can't, execute the hit-and-run.

Gil Hodges waits with his catcher as a pitching change is made.

Richie Ashburn is picked off first, Carl Erskine to Gil Hodges.

The same thing holds true for stealing bases. I would guess that the least appreciated part of baseball is the art of stealing bases. Most people, I feel, think that it's merely a matter of speed, and that isn't true. Speed is an important part of it, certainly. If you run the hundred yards in thirty seconds flat, chances are that you aren't going to be much of a base stealer. But speed alone isn't enough.

To me, the best example is Maury Wills. Now, Wills can run, but when he and I were teammates on the Dodgers there were four or five guys on the club who could probably beat Wills in a hundred-yard dash. (I wasn't one of them.) But none was a better base stealer than Maury. In fact, Wills is the best I've ever seen, and that includes Lou Brock, who certainly rates a close second.

Runners like Brock and Wills rarely, if ever, get a sign to steal. They know better than anyone else what their chances are, and the matter is left up to them. What they do get is a sign *not* to steal. In certain situations, the manager may decide that he doesn't want a Wills or Brock to steal, so he'll flash a sign for the runner not to go.

Some people might wonder how such a situation might come up, so let me explain. The superstealer is on first, with a left-hander pitching. With two out, the batter is a right-hander, and the following batter is left-handed. Suppose the superstealer goes, and makes second safely. First base is now open, so the pitcher doesn't care whether or not he walks the batter, as he'd rather pitch to the next man, anyhow. In certain situations like this, the superstealer might be held at first, in order to force the left-handed pitcher to pitch to the right-handed batter.

One more thought about giving signs. The younger the boy, the simpler the sign. Remember that I said they should be kept simple at the professional level, so how simple can they get? Well, here's a thought. With very young boys, I believe that the signs should be word signs, and given by the manager. A young-

Hodges slides into third to make the most of a hit, a triple. Bubba Phillips waits for the ball.

ster coaching third base has enough to do—concentrating on base runners and keeping his eyes on the defense—without worrying about getting signs from the manager, mixing them in with a lot of decoys, then flashing them on to the runner. Take the responsibility for that yourself when you're managing.

A very simple example of word signs would be to tie up the first letter of the first word with whatever action you want. For example, in a bunt situation, the manager might holler to young Johnny Smith at the plate, "Be alive, Johnny," or some other phrase beginning with the letter "B." Johnny knows that if he hears, "Be ready, Johnny," he's bunting. On the other hand if he hears, "Get ready, Johnny," the manager is just decoying.

If the phrase begins with a "B," Johnny is bunting. If it starts with an "H" ("Have a good eye, Johnny"), the hit-and-run is on. "S" would be the key letter for a steal situation, and "T" for take. You can make your own variations on this, since it's always possible that the opposing manager read this book, too. (That's our big disagreement. You hope he didn't, and I hope he did.)

There are other signs that are used. Squeeze plays, suicide squeeze plays, and so on, but those are better off being explained verbally than trying to go by a sign. Actually, among very young players they're better being ignored altogether.

So much for the offensive meeting, and now to the defensive meeting. Here is where the team gets together to "go over the hitters." Managers explain how they want the batters on the other team pitched, or in some cases, the pitcher conducts the meeting, and tells the rest of the team how he wants the defense lined up for each batter. These meetings are not very helpful below the professional level, in my opinion, because teams don't get to see enough of each other to know the habits of hitters.

Which brings us around to the question of who calls the pitches when the game starts. As I mentioned earlier, I'm in favor of having the catcher do it. It's part of his job, and part of the fun of catching. A manager is going to have enough trouble getting somebody to catch, without telling the catcher that he's not going to be allowed to call the pitches. Though some catchers might rather let you do it, all in all, it's his job.

The lone exception to this would be the pitchout. If you think that the runner might be going to steal, you should have some sort of signal to the catcher that you want a pitchout. Young catchers are often reluctant to call for a pitchout, and it might be advisable for you to take the responsibility. Also, if the pitcher knows that the pitchout sign is coming from the manager, he might be more receptive.

I read that John McGraw once called every pitch for an entire season when he was managing the New York Giants. However, that's an exception. If you insist on calling every pitch, don't complain when your players get very tense. Let *them* play the game, and the mistakes can be talked about the next day.

That doesn't mean that a manager shouldn't make suggestions. As an example, a right-handed batter hits safely to right field the first two times up. The manager might point that out to the catcher, and suggest that the next time up it would be wise to keep the ball inside to that batter, because he obviously prefers the pitch that's out and away from him.

I'm a believer in meetings for young players. Baseball should be something for them to think about, as well as play. But the meetings shouldn't be for the purpose of bawling them out or humiliating them. It should be an opportunity for them to learn. They have questions, and your ability as a manager will be directly related to your ability to answer those questions.

Don't fill their heads full of theory. Football coaches can work out very detailed plays, and basketball coaches can work on play patterns. Baseball, as I said before, is a game where the player *re*acts more than he acts. I could quote a lot of complex thinking about the art of baseball, but I think the best description of all came from Willie Mays.

Willie once described his playing this way: "When somebody throws the ball, I hit it. When somebody hits it, I catch it." Mays is a very knowledgeable ballplayer, and, to me, that quote proves it.

I'm reluctant, for two reasons, to go into a discussion of strategy for players who are very young. For one thing, it often doesn't apply the same way as it does to professionals.

As an example, in most cases I would probably move my outfield around toward right field against a left-handed batter. However, in a Little League game, the exact opposite might be true. Since the pitchers so often overpower the young hitters, the likelihood that the batter will pull the ball is lessened. There's a better chance that the batter will swing late, in which case the outfield should have been moved in the opposite direction.

Along the same line, Little League rules will prevent a manager from making some pitching moves that I might be able to make. The rules for the youngsters spell out how many innings a boy can pitch, so it would be silly for me to talk about moving pitchers in and out unless I was forced to live with such rules.

In the same vein, where I might have a batter taking a pitch, you might be better off letting him swing. He doesn't get to play that often, and it doesn't seem right to deprive him of the best part of the game of baseball—hitting the ball.

The second, and most important, reason is that strategy can deprive kids of the fun of baseball, which is really the only reason for kids to play it. I don't think *every* boy should play baseball, only the ones who enjoy it. By the same token, no one should deprive them of that enjoyment for any reason, least of all strategy.

In closing, let me say one thing to the would-be "genius" managers. It's a lesson that I learned, not as a manager, but as a player. To me, it points up the futility of trying to plan too many things in the game of baseball.

As a young first baseman, I once worked out a play in my

mind. The situation would be a runner on first, and the batter sacrificing. My job was to charge the plate. Sometimes, in this spot, a batter will hit a little pop-up. When that happens, some hitters, instead of running, stand there and smack their bats into the ground.

My plan was this. The next time that happened, I would let the ball drop at my feet. Then I'd pick it up quickly and throw to second. Because the batter had delayed himself to show how unhappy he was, there was a good chance I'd be able to start a double play. Pretty smart, I figured.

The next time I got a chance to use that play was almost three years later. I was a genius, but I was the only one who knew it.

UMPIRES

A MANAGER, AT every level, has to deal with different people. The groups include his players, opposing managers and players, fans, sometimes the press, and always, the umpires. The relationship between a manager and the men who will umpire his games can be very important, and for many different reasons.

Over the years, I've had relations with umpires that could fit just about every kind of description, from "friendly" to "cool." As a player, I had excellent relations with them. One thing that contributed to that, I think, was a story that got a lot of publicity. It happened also to be true.

One day, in Ebbets Field, I was called out on strikes. When I got back to the bench, the Dodgers manager Charley Dressen said to me, "Where was that last pitch?" I told him that I thought the ball was outside, and I started to walk over to sit down. Now

Washington Senators manager Gil Hodges and pitcher Steve Ridzik charge
screaming at home-plate umpire Bill Stewart in the bottom of the twelfth
inning at Yankee Stadium on July 15, 1965. Catcher Doug Camilli joins
in the protest. Umpire Stewart ruled that relief pitcher Ridzik nicked
Yankee batter Clete Boyer with a pitch with the bases filled to force in a
run and give New York a 2 to 1 win. The protest, as usual, was to no avail.

Charley started to holler. "Why didn't you tell *him* what you thought?" I mumbled something about it not doing any good.

Finally, Charley said: "If you don't say anything, they're going to keep giving those pitches to the pitcher. You've got to speak up. If you'll get on one of those guys, I'll give you fifty dollars. Holler at him, say *something* to him, and it's worth fifty to you." The whole idea seemed so ridiculous to me that I finally grinned and said, "How about if I don't ask him how his wife and kids are?" Charley just threw up his hands, and walked away.

We were playing the Braves that day, and shortly after Charley had gotten on me, we were in the field. Eddie Stanky got on first base, and we tried a pick-off play. I thought we got Stanky, but Umpire Bill Stewart didn't. I got into quite a discussion with Stewart trying to convince him that he was wrong, but of course it didn't do any good.

Meantime, back on the bench, Charley sent the bat boy into the clubhouse to get a fifty-dollar bill. When the inning ended, and I went back to our bench, Charley was standing there with the fifty in his hand. He said to me, "Here, take it. You did what I told you to do." I just shook my head, and Charley said, "Can't you use fifty?" I said, "Yes, Charley, I can use it, but I don't want it to become a habit."

At the time, I just couldn't understand Charley's thinking. Now that I'm a manager, I understand it. I don't agree with it, but I do understand it. My record with umpires isn't as good as it was when I was playing, but I really don't have much trouble with them.

I recognize that the biggest part of that is just the way I am. Whether I'm right or wrong, it's the way I've been brought up, and it's an area where I don't feel any desire to change. It's tough to put into words. It's just that, no matter what some people might think, umpires *are* human beings.

I don't know how many different men have umpired games

that I played in or managed in the big leagues. Maybe eighty or ninety, all told. But one thing I can tell you, for sure. They were all different.

Let me give you some examples of what they were like, and I'll use names that some people might be familiar with.

First, though, I'd better say that the one they still talk about most, the late Bill Klem, had retired before I came to the Dodgers. I met him because he was the supervisor of National League umpires when I broke in, and I've heard so many stories about him from the older guys that I feel I knew him better than I did.

I heard him tell a story one time that I never forgot, I guess because it had to do with the way that coal miners take their baseball. I grew up around miners, so I appreciated it.

It seems that when Mr. Klem was breaking in, he was the first umpire to crouch behind the catcher, instead of standing straight up. One day, in Pittsburgh, the Pirates bench was getting on him. When he'd crouch, the Pittsburgh players would start hooting at him. He warned them a couple of times to stop, but they kept it up. Finally, he walked over to the bench and told them that if it didn't stop, he'd clear everyone out. Well, it didn't stop, and Mr. Klem was a man of his word. He chased all of them.

In from left field, on the dead run, came the Pittsburgh manager, Fred Clarke. Clarke wanted to know what the trouble was, and Mr. Klem told him. Clarke said, "What happens now if one of my players gets hurt? You've thrown all the substitutes out." Mr. Klem said, "Mr. Manager, if one of your players gets hurt, the game is over." (In those days, that was the rule.)

Clarke looked at his bench, and the only one sitting there was a nine-year-old bat boy. Then the manager looked back at the umpire and, pointing to the boy, said, "What do you want me to do with *him*?" Mr. Klem said he couldn't care less about the boy, but Clarke said, "Well, I'll get rid of him for you, too."

With that he walked over grabbed the youngster by the scruff of the neck, pointed at the umpire, and gave the boy a boot in the seat of his pants, and sent him off the field. Then the manager trotted back to his position in left field.

Mr. Klem said: "Can you imagine what a going-over I got? It was a holiday, and the Pittsburgh park was full of coal miners. As far as they knew, I had ordered that little boy thrown out of the park. They gave me an afternoon I never forgot."

But let's get back to some of the umpires I had experience with. We can start with "Beans" Reardon. Beans had a high-pitched voice, and he didn't mind using it. He was different in a couple of ways. For one thing, he always wore an outside chest protector, at a time when everyone else in the league wore the inside model. Another thing about him was the way he reacted to being cussed. Most umpires would chase a player when the player cussed him, but Beans would cuss them back. With Beans, you could count on two things. You *would* get a fair shake, and you *wouldn't* get the last word.

Jocko Conlan was another one with a high-pitched voice. He also wanted the last word, but he wouldn't swear at a player or manager, and he wouldn't let anyone swear at him. The fans seemed to like Jocko, probably because he always put it on for them a little. He was a bantam-rooster type, who could tell you a joke one minute, and throw you out of the game the next.

Babe Pinelli was very quiet as an umpire, although they tell me he was a rough one to handle when he was a player. Babe was easy to talk to, and very slow to chase anybody. I remember one day before a game in Brooklyn, we were standing near the batting cage, and the subject got around to umpires. Somebody started talking about who was the least likely to throw you out of a game.

There were several names mentioned, but Pee Wee Reese held out for Pinelli, while Jackie Robinson and a couple of others voted for other umpires. The reason I remember it so well was

that Reese was thrown out of the game in the first inning that day
—by Pinelli.

It's tough for me to discuss umpires, and not mention Al
Barlick. But Al's umpiring in the league I'm working in, and
he might be chasing me while you're reading this. Still, I can't
leave him out. He bears down as hard on his job as a man
possibly could. He's very serious on the field, perhaps sometimes
too serious. But I have to say that I don't think I've ever seen
a better umpire in my life.

Now, I know that I'm leaving out a lot of men. But the men
who are working in the National League and American League
now, with the exception of Barlick, I've omitted on purpose. I
don't think anything that I might say about them would make
them lean over one inch for me, but some people might mis-
understand. I hope it's enough to say that their job is a tough
one and that baseball is very fortunate to have the umpires it has.

I've left out some of the others who have retired or passed
on, mostly because of space. But I don't use the word loosely
when I say that I'm proud to have known them, and proud to
have gotten along with them.

I have to confess that I did have one umpire who might be
described as a "favorite," the late Larry Goetz. Larry was a
good storyteller, with a wonderful sense of humor. But when he
was on the field, he was an umpire. He was the boss. You could
joke with Larry, and he'd seem to enjoy it. But somehow you
never forgot that he was the man in charge.

Maybe my best memory of Larry in action came during the
seventh game of the 1952 World Series. I came up in the eighth
inning with one out, and the Yankees leading, 4 to 2. Bob
Kuzava was pitching. Goetz told me later that he hadn't slept a
wink the night before, knowing that he would be working behind
the plate in the seventh game. It was a pressure spot, and he
knew it.

Anyway, I took a pitch, and Larry called it a strike. I didn't

A double view of a controversial call in the 1952 World Series between the Yanks and the Dodgers. Umpire Art Passarella called pinch-hitter Johnny Sain out, but these pictures indicate that Hodges' foot was forced off the bag as Sain flew across the base. There was a great uproar from the fans as well as from Coach Bill Dickey (33). The Dodgers won the game in the eleventh inning, 6 to 5.

A difference of opinion. Manager Hodges argues with Umpire Emmett Ashford.

say anything, but our bench started to grumble. Finally, Ralph Branca yelled, "Hodges didn't miss the pitch, Goetz. You did." Well, just that quickly, Larry's mask came off, he spun around, pointed at Branca, and said, "Well, I'm not going to miss *you*. Get out of there." That's why Ralph missed the last inning and a half of that World Series.

Judge Samuel Leibowitz was a big fan of the Dodgers, and the players and the umpires got to know him. One day, he ran into Larry coming into Ebbets Field, and they started talking. Judge Leibowitz finally said, "You know, Larry, your job and mine are a lot alike." Goetz looked at him for a minute, and said, "Judge, when you get a tough one to decide, you take it into your chambers to think about it for a while. With me, I've got thirty thousand wolves hollering that they want it right now. Another thing, you say to some punk, 'Seven and a half to fifteen in the state penitentiary,' and he says 'Thank you, your Honor.' I say 'Strike two,' and they call me names you've never heard. No, Judge, the jobs aren't really that much alike."

Now that we've talked about umpires that I've known, let's take a look at the ones that all managers meet. A good thing for any manager, or any umpire, to keep in mind is something that Larry Goetz used to say. Larry's philosophy was: "I know that there are a lot of ballplayers who don't like me. I couldn't care less. I'm not one bit interested in their affection. What I *do* want is their respect."

Umpires are entitled to that respect. It's a tough job, done under difficult conditions. Did you ever stop to think that a home-plate umpire makes about 250 decisions a game, and doesn't have any time to deliberate on any of them. He's going to make mistakes. There's no way he can avoid it. He knows that he's going to make them, too, but he tries hard not to.

Let's take the case of an imaginary shortstop. You can find him anywhere from the Little League to the major leagues. He gets a double-play ball in his glove, and drops it. Later on, he makes a bad throw. He fails to cover second base when he should. At bat, the first time up he strikes out on a ball that bounces in front of the plate. The next time up, he swings late, bloops a ball over the first baseman's head for a base hit, then gets picked off first. The third time up, he takes a pitch that's an inch off the plate, and when it's called a strike, he jumps all over the umpire.

What makes it even worse is that as long as he doesn't talk too long, or get too abusive, the umpire has to listen to it. You'd better believe they've got a tough job.

As I said, umpires are human. They all have a philosophy that once the ball game is over, everything should be forgotten. Tomorrow is a brand-new day. It's a great philosophy, but it doesn't always work that way. Players don't always forget. Neither do managers. And, being perfectly honest, neither do umpires. I had an argument with an umpire one day, and the next day when I showed up at home plate with the lineup card, I said hello to him. He turned his back on me. That's wrong. Holding a grudge is a luxury that neither a manager nor an umpire can afford.

It's part of a manager's job to see to it that his players don't carry grudges, and to do what he can about seeing that umpires don't carry grudges against his players. It leads to more than just small arguments. It leads to players being thrown out of ball games, and that hurts the whole ball club.

In the same area, it's the manager's responsibility to keep order on the bench. Jockeying is a part of the game, but it's the job of the manager to see that it doesn't go too far. When it comes to umpires, it doesn't accomplish a thing worthwhile. Not only that, but it can be dangerous.

Let's imagine that you've got a good pinch hitter on the bench. Somebody starts to holler at the umpire, and he doesn't know who it is. He's got to guess. If he guesses wrong, that pinch hitter might be in the clubhouse when you need him.

Most important of all, I feel, is the confrontation between the manager and the umpire. Sometimes it's got to happen. It just can't be avoided. The time comes when you've got to get off that bench, and have a little discussion.

Let me first discuss the problem at the Little League level. A manager might run screaming to the umpire, use the foulest language he can, and abuse the umpire until he runs out of breath. That same night, that Little League manager might be standing around at a cocktail party and loudly worrying about why the youth of today has no respect for authority.

If you're managing a team of youngsters, you have to set an example. The phrase "character builder" seems to be going out of style. But to be perfectly honest, I don't think a manager or a coach of a team of youngsters can really do his job unless he includes that part of it. If he's not prepared to set an example for his players, he's a bad coach or manager, no matter how much he knows about baseball.

To get back again to the necessity of knowing your players. If you've got a youngster on your team who's a hothead, and you see him get tangled up with an umpire, get out there. If the boy is right or wrong, he needs you. It's your job to turn the screaming contest into a discussion, and the best way to do it is to substitute yourself for the player.

Now, I'm not saying that a player isn't entitled to ask about a decision. What I'm saying is that he has no right to be abusive. Or, to take another side of it, he has a responsibility to stay in the game. You put him in the lineup because you thought he could help the team win. He's not going to be much help sitting in the clubhouse.

At the professional level, the same theories hold true, but they're a lot harder to put into effect. On the other hand, there are punishments available to professionals with bad tempers that aren't there with the kids.

Umpires don't like to be shown up. Neither does anyone else that I can think of. If you remember that, you've got a better chance of getting your story over to an umpire. You probably won't win, but you cut down your chances of being chased. I can't think of a more valuable tip than this—keep your hands in your pockets.

Umpires don't care too much for having managers hollering and waving their arms. As they say, "It looks bad." They're right. Don't show him up with gestures. If you think he missed a play, tell him quietly. Think about it this way. What would you do if one of your players booted a ball and the umpires ridiculed him with gestures. You'd want the umpire thrown out of the park. Well, it works two ways.

Remember, too, that umpires work differently. You'll get a better job out of most of them if you don't holler at them. I can recall a time when the Dodgers were having trouble with an ex-pitcher turned umpire, Lon Warneke. One night, Warneke was due to work behind the plate, and one of our coaches, Clyde Sukeforth, suggested that instead of getting on Warneke, the whole club keep quiet.

We did it, too. After the game, everybody agreed that Warneke had done a great job. It was simple, really. An umpire has to concentrate to do a good job. Nobody can concentrate with a lot of people hollering at him. Some umpires will work with one eye on the bench when they're being heckled, and you need to use both eyes to umpire a good game.

There are other umpires who seem determined to call attention to themselves. That's their mistake. Mr. Klem used to say that the greatest applause an umpire can get is silence, and there's a lot to that.

Let me give you a good example of what I mean. Without a doubt, the biggest game I ever played in my life was the final game of the 1951 playoff against the Giants. That's the game where Bobby Thomson hit his famous home run. It's a day that none of us will ever forget who were in the game, much as some of us would like to.

A couple of years ago a friend of mine asked some questions of some of us. He asked what was the first pitch to Thomson when he came up, and all of us remembered that it was a strike. Then he said, "Who said it was a strike?" He wanted the name of the umpire who was behind the plate that day.

He asked me. He asked Jackie Robinson. He asked Ralph Branca, who was pitching. He asked Rube Walker, who was catching. He asked Bobby Thomson himself. Not a single one of us came up with the right answer. Save yourself a trip to the record books. It was Lou Jorda.

Lou was a nice man, who died several years ago. It's typical of the odd kind of code that umpires have to live by that Lou Jorda would probably be complimented if he knew that we didn't remember that he worked that game. And he *should* feel complimented.

In the event that you might get drafted into umpiring a kid's game, there are some things that it might be well to keep in mind. For one thing, make your decisions firmly. Convince the youngsters that you're sure, even if you're not. If you're indecisive, it doesn't make any difference if you're right or wrong, you're going to get a complaint. In fairness to the kids, the same thing is true in the major leagues.

Don't try to influence the outcome of the game. Now, I'm not accusing you of dishonesty when I say that. Sometimes, though, there's a tendency to try to "even things up" when kids are playing. Baseball is the kind of game that can take care of that by itself. If you do it, you'll run a good chance of losing the respect of the kids, and probably wind up kicking yourself for doing it. Just let things happen.

As for juvenile tempers flaring up, about the only advice I can give you is to know how you're going to break up the fight. Don't grab one boy, but get between them and push them apart. If you grab one kid, you're making him a target for the other one. Also, when you've got it under control, try to get the two youngsters to shake hands. Chances are, you'll be successful, which just goes to show that kids are often smarter than adults.

When it comes to discipline, put the matter right up to the two managers before the game starts. If they can't handle their players, it's unreasonable to expect you to do it. An umpire runs the same risk that a manager does, in that he shouldn't take the game away from the kids. But, in a way, I feel that warning is really unnecessary. Only a man who really cares for youngsters would volunteer to umpire one of their ball games.

Sometimes it might be good to remember the kind of men that umpires are. Years ago, the famous cartoonist Willard Mullin drew a cartoon about Bill Klem. It was a series of drawings, connected by a parody on "Gunga Din." A friend of mine has the original of that drawing, given to him by Mr. Klem, and the last part of it reads:

> "For it's Klem! Klem! Klem!
> You blind, ol', thievin' robber, Mister Klem.
> Though they've blasted you and flayed you,
> By the livin' Gawd that made you,
> You're a better man than they are, Mister Klem.

It's something to think about.

KIDS

WHAT IS BASEBALL? Obviously, there are a lot of different answers to that question. To some people it's relaxation; to some it's excitement; and to some it's a bore. To me, it's a way of life; it's the method of supporting my family; it's a profession that's been enjoyable and rewarding to me.

But to kids it's a game. It's fun. An adult who gives of himself to bring that game to youngsters has done something of which he can be very proud. The adult who becomes involved, however, and in so doing deprives youngsters of that fun, is guilty of a crime, as far as I'm concerned.

There has been a tremendous change in the past twenty years or so, as far as youngsters playing baseball is concerned. I grew up at a time when parents sent their boys out to play baseball the same way they sent them to school or to the grocery store.

129

They just opened the door, and let them go. Today, that's all changed. The parents are a part of the youngster's baseball life. They go to the games; they even coach and manage the teams. The mothers make the uniforms.

Maybe that's good; maybe it isn't. I mentioned earlier in this book that I'm not a psychiatrist. I'll leave the problem to them. My father had limited opportunities to see my brother or me play baseball when we were kids. He was working in a mine so that we'd get the chance to play. When Bob and I were old enough to work in mine shafts ourselves, my father wouldn't let us. He encouraged us to play baseball instead. He never let us forget that he was working in the mines so we wouldn't have to.

Perhaps I might have enjoyed baseball more as a youngster if my father had been able to see me play more often. Perhaps I wouldn't have enjoyed it as much. I guess the really important thing is that when he wasn't there, I knew why.

My father lived long enough to see me play in the major leagues. He even saw me play in a World Series. In that respect, I've been lucky. But, in a selfish way, I guess, I wish he could have lived long enough to see one more thing.

It's on McDonald Avenue and Shell Road in Brooklyn, which is a long way from southern Indiana, in more measurements than just miles. It's in an area where there are plenty of kids, but where there isn't a lot of room for them to play baseball. It's a ball park, and it's a dandy.

It has two ball fields, a concrete grandstand, a clubhouse, dressing rooms with lockers, lavatories and showers. There are water fountains in the dugouts, sprinkler and drainage systems on the field, and lights all around the park. It provides a place to play for five hundred boys who make up the South Highway Little League. I wish my father could have seen all this, and the sign that says "Gil Hodges Stadium."

During my career, I've been fortunate enough to pick up some awards. Don't get me wrong: I haven't had to build any exten-

sions on my house to make room for them, but there have been
some. I can honestly say that every one was appreciated, but
just as honestly, I have to say that nothing has given me the same
degree of pride that I get every time I see that field. I just wish
that my father was able to share that feeling with me.

Let's get one thing straight. I didn't put that field there. That
was done by a lot of dedicated men, including one of my dearest
friends, Sid Loberfeld. Sid is an attorney, and maybe someday
he'll write a book of his own about the things he's done for the
kids in Brooklyn. It would be a thicker book than this one, and
what makes him so special is that it would probably be the first
time that a lot of those kids ever heard his name.

As Sid would be quick to admit, these aren't one-man jobs.
There were people like Bernard Schaefer, former president of
the League, and Ben Fazio, the current president. There were
city officials who cooperated so much, like Commissioner Joseph
E. O'Grady, Commissioner John J. Gilhooley, the Honorable
Walter L. Schlager, and the Honorable John J. Quinn. Then there
were people who gave up so much of their free time, including
nights and weekends, just to make sure that this field became
a reality.

While I was managing the Washington club, I naturally didn't
get much chance to stop by the field. But now that I pass it on
my way to Shea Stadium when the Mets are at home, I like to
drop in and watch the kids play, and maybe help out with a
suggestion or two to the boys. I'm on my way to a place where
baseball is also a job, and it's a big kick to stop for moment at
a place where it's just fun.

I've mentioned a lot of these things not only because they're
important to me but also so that I can make my position on
Little League quite clear. I like it, and I believe in it. But, like
a lot of other things that I like and believe in, there are some
things that I wish were different. For a few moments, let's take a
look at some of them.

Batting instruction at Gil Hodges Stadium. Sid Loberfeld, prominent New York attorney and counsel to the Little League, holds the microphone.

Another enterprise in which Hodges is interested is Gil Hodges Lanes, in Brooklyn. This picture, taken at the opening of the bowling alleys in February, 1961, shows from the left: Joe Pignatano, Bobby Aspromonte, Sid Gordon, Bobby Giallombardo, Whitey Ford, and Gil. Hodges is associated in this enterprise with his friend and family physician, Dr. Anthony S. Terranova.

Since we are dealing primarily with managers, let's examine the Little League manager. (I should stop right here, I suppose, and apologize to Little League. The Little League program has been so successful in this country, that all youth programs are described that way, whether or not they're affiliated with Little League Baseball, Inc. For the most part here, I'll be talking about all boys' baseball programs.)

Managing a kids' baseball team is a tough job. In certain areas, it's tougher than managing a professional team. Some of the problems come from the kids themselves, but that's part of being a kid. Others come from parents, and that's too bad, because in many of those cases the real loser turns out to be the boy himself. Also, there are problems that the manager makes for himself.

The importance of the manager is underlined in the 1968 *Handbook* of Little League Baseball, Inc. Included in the handbook is an excerpt from a study and analysis of the manager's role by Dr. Arthur A. Esslinger, Past President, American Association for Health, Physical Education and Recreation, and a member of the Board of Directors of Little League Baseball. Here's part of what Dr. Esslinger says:

"The heart of Little League Baseball is what happens between manager and boy. It is your manager more than any other single individual who makes your program a success or failure. He controls the situation in which the players may be benefited or harmed. We have all seen managers who exerted a wonderful influence upon their boys—an influence which was as fine an educational experience as any lad might undergo. Unfortunately, we have also observed a few managers who were a menace to children.

"If Little League is to become qualitative then we must do something positive about improving the quality of leadership in its day-to-day operation. This assignment is made more difficult by two factors. The first of these is that we lose many of our experienced personnel every year. Many men stay in the program as long as their sons are in it. Then, when they have gained invaluable experience, and acquired some of the ideals of the program, we lose them. What would be the quality of teaching in our schools if our teachers turned over as rapidly as our managers?"

Doctor Esslinger finishes this way:

"Little League has had many managers of the finest caliber. It is often surprising that we have had as many excellent managers as we have had. But despite our good managers, we are all forced to admit that we have had too many poor ones. Many have done harm to their players and have given critics an opportunity to blast our program. They constitute the greatest threat to our program. Our procedures in regard to managers is the Achilles heel of Little League Baseball.

"We have stimulated the imaginations of a million boys to come into this program. Yet for their leadership we have largely trusted to the luck of the draw—to mere accident. The least we can do for all these youngsters is to try to find them a good manager, and, once selected, provide him with some indoctrination and in-service training. This, it seems to me, is a solemn obligation. The quality of leadership represents our biggest problem and until we solve it we can never realize the full potential we have."

It seems to me that Dr. Esslinger has made some good points. I'm not sure that I understand his feelings about the role of the manager, though. If he's talking about more control of the youngsters, I honestly feel that he'd be better off going the other way. I'd rather see managers instructed on how to make the game more enjoyable for the boys, instead of how to conform more to the guidelines of an organized program.

One area that I think is abused is the position of Little League baseball as stepping-stone to the major leagues. It's not, any more than students are taught French in our schools to prepare them to live in France. It's merely an outlet for some kids to have fun.

At the American Baseball Academy in New York, in 1951, Gil Hodges shows youngsters how to play first base. The school was started by Phil Rizzuto, and its faculty also included Gene Woodling and Sid Gordon.

At Gil Hodges Stadium in Brooklyn, in 1968, Hodges instructs Little Leaguers.

I hear about parents and managers who say that a youngster is a "cinch" to become a professional player. My answer to that is simple. I have spent my life in professional baseball. I've been fortunate enough to work for some of the finest minds in the game, including the late Branch Rickey. I don't believe that I, or anyone up to, and including, Mr. Rickey, can look at a twelve-year-old ballplayer and tell you that he can become a professional, let alone a major leaguer.

There are players in the big leagues now who couldn't make their high school teams. Players who come out of college and get bonuses in six figures sometimes fail to last a single season of pro ball. The ability to estimate the potential of a fully grown youngster is tough enough. To make that kind of judgment on a twelve-year-old is, in my estimation, impossible.

There are too many factors to consider. A good example of one of those factors can be found in a statement by a great Hall-of-Fame pitcher, Burleigh Grimes. After playing and managing in the big leagues, Grimes became a scout, and a good one. He was looking at youngsters who were ready to graduate from high school or who were of college age. Grimes said, "If I could look inside of their heads, I might never make a mistake." In effect, he was saying that he could see their physical attributes, but their minds were also a factor in success or failure as professional players.

Along this line, there's a tendency on the part of a lot of men who manage boys' teams to overmanage. While it's understandable that the kids might want to imitate their favorite players, it doesn't make sense for the managers to try to emulate a man who's handling a big-league club. They're doing different kinds of things, because they're working for different results.

Let's take a hypothetical situation. It's the last inning, and my team is losing, 10 to 4. (After managing second-division teams for as long as I have, I'm familiar with this kind of situation.) The count on my first batter of the inning goes to 3 to 0.

Chances are that I'm going to give him a sign to take the next pitch. I have to get men on base. I have a six-run deficit to overcome. If I let him swing, and he hits a home run, I'm still five runs behind. If he takes a pitch, and it's a strike, he's still ahead of the pitcher.

Now, let's imagine that I'm managing a kid's team. I think I'd probably leave the boy on his own. Chances are that he'll get a pitch he can handle, and if he does, why shouldn't he swing? He's there to have some fun, and the best fun in baseball is hitting the ball. At the high school level, American Legion baseball, or in college, then the youngster should be taking some kind of orders. But a Little Leaguer should have the emphasis on fun.

The thinking here is that the more a youngster gets to enjoy baseball, the more of its workings he'll learn himself. On the other hand, he's not going to make much effort to learn about something that he doesn't like. Some Little Leaguers, in the kind of spot just mentioned, will take the pitch on their own. That would seem to indicate a knowledge of baseball, and, in turn, a liking for it.

A situation like that one brings up a thought. For a boy to learn when to swing and when not to swing, the first thing he must do is learn the strike zone. Here's a thought that might help a Little League manager in that area. Try to have a batting practice session every so often, where the batter doesn't swing at the ball.

That might sound silly, but let me give you an example of what I mean. Suppose a team shows up on the day after a rainstorm, and the field is unplayable, even though the rain has stopped. Don't let everyone go home. Instead, fix up the mound and the batters' boxes so they can be used. Then have your pitchers throw, but don't let the batters swing.

Instead, have them just stand there and holler either "Strike" or "Ball," depending on what they thought the umpire might call the pitch. You stand behind the backstop, and watch. By this method, a manager might find out that he can help some of his young hitters by teaching them to study the strike zone more closely. Know the strike zone, concentrate on contact, and you become a better hitter. That, in turn, will make baseball more fun.

Which brings us around to the thing that really makes hitting difficult—pitching. It seems to me that there's no balance between hitting and pitching in Little League. More and more, it's becoming a pitcher's game. To me, a kid's game where the score is 1 to 0, and both pitchers strike out seventeen men, is a waste of time.

Let's examine what happens. Neither club's hitters get much chance to hit the ball or to field it. About the only ones who get anything out of the game are the two pitchers. An occasional game like that is bound to happen. But if it happens too frequently, it's wrong. There are eighteen youngsters on a field looking for some fun, and only two of them are having it.

How to bring the pitching down to the level of the hitting is a tough problem. If a boy is a good pitcher, and he can throw hard, and throw strikes, it doesn't seem right to penalize him. But sometimes it isn't just the fast ball that he throws. Sometimes it's the curve, and there lies one of the great faults of Little League Baseball.

Shortly before the end of the 1967 season, I was sitting in my office one day with our pitching coach, Rube Walker. Rube and I were teammates in Brooklyn, and a lot of the success that the Mets have had with young pitching is attributable to Rube. He's a man who's made a study of pitching, and learned it thoroughly.

As we were talking, the subject got around to Little League, and especially the use of the curve ball. Rube said: "If I had a son, and he was pitching Little League ball, I'd tell him *never* to throw a curve ball. I'd tell him that for a lot of reasons, but the biggest one is that he's got a great chance of hurting his arm." I agreed with Rube 100 percent.

Now, that brings us back to what I said earlier about the Little Leagues not being a proving ground for big leaguers. I'm not worried, and neither is Rube, about the potential ruining of a big-league pitcher. We both feel that a kid should get a chance to pitch in high school or college. His ability to pitch might never make a career for him, but it might get him an education. A curve ball is so wrong for kids of that age that I would seriously recommend to Little League that the pitch be outlawed.

I say that not only because of its damage to a young arm but also because it destroys the fun in the game for the kids who can't hit it. Kids today in Little League are pretty big; some of them are around six feet. Usually, the biggest guys get to pitch, because they throw harder. They've got a big enough edge with a fast ball. The curve only makes things worse.

Again, it isn't only the hitters who suffer. Infielders and out-fielders don't get a chance to handle the ball because there are so many kids being struck out. By giving the pitcher a tremen-dous edge, batters lose interest in playing baseball. After all, nothing kills interest like continuous failure. As a result, baseball interest, which should be reaching its peak, dies at the age of eleven or twelve. Part of the blame for that belongs to the curve ball.

It occurs to me that I might sound like someone who's saying: "Tell the kids not to care about winning. Just go out and make all the mistakes in the world, have a good time, and forget about whether or not you win." If I do sound like that, I apologize. Nothing could be further from what I'm trying to say.

Certainly winning is important. If a youngster isn't trying to win, then he's not really playing baseball. He might just as well not play, as play without caring about winning. What I'm hoping to emphasize is that winning should be kept in perspective.

One of the most successful leaders in the world of sport is the former coach of the Boston Celtics, Red Auerbach. Red got a lot of mileage out of a quote that went "Show me a good loser—

and I'll show you a loser." To me, that belongs with Leo Durocher's "Nice guys finish last." They're both good phrases, but I don't really believe either one of them. I'll go further than that—I don't believe that Auerbach or Durocher really believe them, either.

Losing is a part of life. If you ever get to where you like to lose, you're in a lot of trouble. But if you don't learn to live with it, you're in just as much trouble, maybe more. Baseball, particularly, teaches people to live with losing, and the more you play, the more familiar you get. A football player might have an undefeated season, but never a professional baseball player.

Let's look at losing for a minute. Back in the days when they played in the Polo Grounds, the Giants had a player who got himself a reputation as "a fierce competitor." He was often referred to as "a hard loser." These things were meant as compliments.

One day, the Giants lost a tough game. When it was over, this player came into the clubhouse, and sat dejectedly in front of his locker. Suddenly he jumped up, took his uniform shirt in both hands, and tore it in half. Then he picked up his uniform pants, grabbed a leg with each hand, and tore the pants in two. Sitting to one side was Herman Franks, later to manage the team in San Francisco, but then a coach. Franks walked over to the player, and said: "I've heard about you guys who are hard losers, and I just wanted to ask you something. Do you guys ever get mad enough to rip up your *own* clothes?"

I can hear some people, people who have read about my sweet disposition in the papers, say: "It's easy for Hodges to talk. He doesn't ever get that worked up about losing, so he pops off about the guys who do." Well, I don't want to spoil my so-called "image," but I can assure you that Mr. Hodges isn't always that calm and serene.

When I was managing the Washington club, we played a game one day in Detroit. I'll spare you the gruesome details; just let me say that we had it won twice, and wound up losing it. Remember that. The Tigers didn't win; we lost it, with some baseball that would make you wonder if a major-league club could be that bad. When the game was over, the first one in the clubhouse was calm, serene Gil Hodges.

In Detroit, they have little stools in front of each locker. The Detroit club announced later that they were sending a bill to the Senators because the manager had broken seven of those stools. I can't honestly say that the bill was ever sent, because I don't know. I do know one thing, though. They were entitled to the money.

I can say to you, in complete honesty, that I mention this only to show that I can understand people who lose their cool when they blow a ball game. But I also have to say that I'm ashamed of what I did that day. I don't just regret it; I'm ashamed of it. It proved nothing; it changed nothing; and it pointed up the logic of something that was told to me years ago about another player.

This player, whom we'll call Jones, was regarded as a very smart baseball man. During his playing days, he was often mentioned as a potential manager. (To give you a good reason why we're calling him Jones, the player *did* eventually become a manager.) But he also had a reputation as a hothead. He was the kind who broke bats, cracked helmets, and had occasional temper tantrums.

Once, when a certain managerial job opened up, there was a lot of speculation that Jones might get it. He didn't. Several months later I overheard a conversation that included the general manager of that club. Somebody asked him why Jones hadn't gotten the job, and the general manager said that Jones hadn't even been considered. Then he said, "How can I expect him to be able to control other people, when he can't even control himself?"

It seems to me that that's even more important at the Little League level than it is in the big leagues. A Little League manager should try to remember that example is probably the biggest thing that he has to offer these kids. After all, hardly any of those boys will be professional ballplayers when they grow up, but all of them will be men.

Getting back to the subject of losing, it's something that should be avoided, but not at *all* costs. If a pitcher, say, is going badly, he should be relieved. It's only fair to the other members of the team that they shouldn't be penalized because he's having a bad day. Now, it would be silly for me to tell a Little League manager how to handle a situation like that. They know their kids, and how the kids react, a lot better than I do. But if I can make a suggestion, it's a matter that should be discussed with pitchers before the season even starts. They might be told that they have to expect that kind of day. Such days happen to Bob Gibson, to Sandy Koufax, to every great pitcher. The stars learned to live with it, so the kids had better learn the same lesson.

If I had to pick one area where a Little League manager could do the most for a potential professional ballplayer, I'd have to say that it would be in the prevention of alibiing. A Little League manager who discourages kids from becoming what Ring Lardner called "Alibi Ikes" is making a tremendous contribution to the youngster. A lot of kids who are otherwise fine young men have a tendency to alibi about what happens to them on a ball field.

As an example, a kid is called out on strikes. He comes back to the bench moaning about how the umpire was blind, crazy, or dishonest. That should be discouraged. How? Well, the next time the kid gets a base on balls, ask him if the umpire missed that call, too. Or let's say a kid hits a ball hard, and it's caught. If he moans too loud or too long, wait until the next time he doesn't mean to swing, but the ball hits his bat and falls in for a base hit.

Now, I'm not saying that a kid isn't entitled to a moment of unhappiness about striking out or getting a hard-hit ball caught.

I'm only talking here about the kid who makes a habit of coming up with an alibi every time things don't go his way.

Here, again, we get into the area of setting an example. If the manager is a "whiner," he can forget about trying to teach the players not to whine. If he explodes, he's not in much of a position to get on the youngsters when they do it.

Because they're dealing with youngsters, Little League managers have special problems in dealing with the problem of losing. So do the youngsters' parents. Al Rosen, formerly a great third baseman with the Cleveland Indians, has written an excellent book on that subject called *Baseball and Your Boy*. In it he talks about the fact that youngsters know when they're being "conned." He points out that if you tell a boy he had a good day, when he really had a bad one, he knows you're not being honest with him. Also, don't tell him that losing the game isn't important, because to the youngster it *is* important. Instead, Rosen has several suggested approaches to the subject.

In the book, Rosen writes: "I have said that the major objective of a Little League is to provide fun for the youngsters. I believe it strongly, and nothing should be allowed to get in the way of that objective. But I think the boy can get a lot more out of it, including an introduction to the hard facts of life. He learns that nature creates great inequalities. On a team of fifteen boys, one or possibly two will have marked ability. The others struggle to acquire what seems to come effortlessly to their gifted teammates. It will not be much different for the rest of their lives. If they start out to be lawyers, or doctors, or scientists, there will always be a few in the group with rare, glittering talent.

"I do not feel sorry for the ordinary ones, which includes almost everybody. There are compensations in learning early what it means to have to scrap and scuffle for everything you get. I learned to live within my limitations as a ballplayer, and I saw others who were like me. Because we were realistic about our failings, we did the obvious things in working hard to offset them. But we developed something else more valuable that is difficult to define in words. It might be called a state of mind, a total concentration, a tenacity of spirit. We came to focus all our attention on the task because we knew it was the only way in which we could get the job done. Discouragement did not throw us off stride simply because it had been our constant companion along the way. Often our mental toughness took us far beyond those who started out with more ability."

I quoted this passage for a purpose. To me, it points up what I think is the greatest kick that can come from managing. When I say that, I include managers at every level from Little League to the big leagues. It's the chance to help a player. Sure, it's nice to have a superstar on your club. I wish I had one. They win ball games for you, and in the position that I'm in, that's the name of the game. But there's a lot that the manager can get from the player who doesn't have the talent of the superstar.

Nobody gets a better shot at this kind of help than the Little League manager. His players come to him without benefit of scouting reports; hence there are no preconceived ideas. He gets to form his own opinions on what he sees. What he'll see, most of the time, is a boy who has a problem in baseball, or even a lot of problems. Often, he won't be able to help the youngster. But sometimes he will, and when he does, the kick that he gets will be tremendous.

Let's say that little Johnny Jones isn't a very good player. Even so, Johnny is a member of the team. The easy way, and the unfair way, is to forget about Johnny altogether. But there's another way. Find something that Johnny *can* do. If he can't run or throw or hit or field, maybe he can bunt. When a bunt situation comes up, have Johnny ready. Let Johnny know that his job is to bunt. Let him practice it. Let him know that his is an important contribution to the team. Sooner or later, you'll get into a situation where that bunt is needed, and Johnny Jones will come through for you. When he does, one look at his face will make it all more than worthwhile.

One of the things that makes managing a Little League team so tough is the fact that the manager can count on being saddled with some players who just can't play very well. It's a problem that he faces, and his best move is to find some way in which he can make these players feel important. You might turn out to benefit from it on the field, too, because a manager never knows who might turn out to make an important contribution.

Let me give you an example. I was on a Dodger team in 1959 with a left-handed pitcher named Gene Snyder. Chances are that Gene Snyder, as Joe Garagiola likes to say, didn't even make the bubble-gum cards. He appeared in twenty games for us that year, and wound up with a record of one victory and one loss. Because it was his only major-league season, his lifetime record shows only one victory.

But he won that game in 1959. When the pennant race ended, the Dodgers were tied for the lead with the Milwaukee Braves. We beat the Braves in a playoff, then went on to win the World Series from the Chicago White Sox. Each full share in that World Series pot meant $11,231.18, and I was lucky enough to get one of those shares. The point I'm making is that if we hadn't won that one game that Gene Snyder won for us, we wouldn't have been in that World Series. Stan Williams was the winning pitcher in the last game of the playoff, but without Gene Snyder's victory we wouldn't have been in the playoff.

The Little League manager has a chance to help himself, his players, and the whole team by working with the youngster who just doesn't have the talent that the others have. Sometimes there is more than one boy with a problem, so the manager works with all of them. It takes patience, sure, but it can be very rewarding. It calls for work on the part of the player *and* the manager. To-gether, though, they can get the job done. Sometimes.

A group of youngsters at Gil Hodges Stadium, with their mascot, person-able, pretty Carole Schaefer.

When Fred Haney was managing the Braves, he wasn't too pleased with the way Eddie Mathews, the third baseman, handled the slow-hit ground ball. He mentioned to Mathews that he thought Eddie should try it another way. Mathews did. Every day for a week he practiced the play the way Haney wanted it made. Finally, he came to Fred and said, "I just can't get comfortable doing it your way, and I don't feel that I can do it." Haney's answer was, "Eddie, I asked you to try something, and you gave it your best shot. I appreciate that. You go back to doing it the way you were doing it." It was the sensible approach. Every player is not going to be able to make the play the way his manager wants him to. But if the manager makes the suggestion, and the youngster makes the effort, something might come of it. In fact, if it's only that the player and the manager understand each other better, it's been worth it for everyone.

In 1968, when Frank Howard had the best year of his life with the bat, he was nice enough to say that a lot of the credit belonged to me because I had worked with him on some of his problems. I appreciate what Frank said, but the credit belongs to Frank Howard. His problems weren't that hard to see or to diagnose. The hard part was solving them, and what made it hard was that the solution could be found only in a lot of work. I never asked Frank to do anything that he wasn't extremely cooperative about. He wanted to improve, and he worked hard for it. I can say in all honesty that I never had a player who worked any harder than Howard did.

If there is one single part of managing Little League teams that is the most difficult, it often is the job of dealing with parents. Every parent wants his boy to play every game, and very few realize that this isn't always possible. It's a problem in the Little Leagues, and I've seen it become a problem in the major leagues. I played on the same team with a fellow who had a lot of ability, but his father's interference worked against the player all the time, both with the manager and the front office.

At the Little League level, it's especially difficult. For one thing, there are no road trips where the manager can get away from the parents. What's the answer? I don't know. As both a manager and a parent, I can sympathize with both sides. About the only thing that I can think of is a preseason meeting, and the hope that it will lead to an understanding. It might not work, but the next step is one that calls for a psychologist. A manager is putting himself in the position of saying to a parent, "Turn your son over to me; let me make all the decisions." It's tough enough to get that kind of guarantee from a man when you're asking only for his wallet. Imagine when you're asking for something as precious to him as his child.

It's important to remember one thing when you're managing a team of youngsters—kids are, after all, kids. Their reactions are going to be the reactions of kids, and you have to be prepared for it. Let me tell you one of my favorite stories that illustrate this.

The date was October 4, 1955, and that's one day that I'll never forget as long as I live. Like so many other days in my life, I spent it playing baseball. But there was one difference. This was the seventh game of the World Series.

In the fourth inning, I got a single off Tommy Byrne, and drove in Roy Campanella with the first run of the game. In the sixth inning, with the bases loaded, I hit a fly ball that scored Pee Wee Reese with the second run. Other than that, I walked and fouled out to the first baseman. Really doesn't sound like too much, except that those two runs were the only two of the game. Johnny Podres shut out the Yankees, and the Dodgers won their very first world championship.

Well, you can imagine what Brooklyn was like that night. I had a big edge on a lot of the other fellows on the team because my home was in Brooklyn. Besides being fans, a lot of the people were neighbors and friends.

When I got home to change my clothes and go to the victory

party, there was a tremendous crowd around my house. It was very nice, because, as I said, these people were more than just fans; they were also friends. Anyway, I finally got into the house, and I was greeted by my son. Gilly was five at the time. He knew that his daddy was a ballplayer, and there was no way, even at his age, that he couldn't have known we were in a World Series. Not the way things had been around my house for the past week.

As I said, I didn't have the greatest day in the world, but I drove in both runs, and it was obvious that there was a lot of excitement in the neighborhood. Maybe you've wondered what a ballplayer hears from his children when he comes home after a big day. Well, when I walked in the house that day, Gilly was sitting in front of the television. That was a good sign, I figured. He looked up at me, and said, "Gee, Daddy, you just missed 'Captain Midnight.' "

As to the parent, the best suggestion that I can make is to get a copy of Al Rosen's book, which I mentioned earlier. Whether or not your interference destroys something very important to your child may very well depend on your knowledge of the boy, and the problems that he faces as a youngster starting to play baseball.

My own particular criticism of Little League is that the boys don't get to play enough. I think the reason might well be that organized participation programs call for the presence of adults, and time is often hard to come by for them. But the kids should be encouraged not only to be a part of a national program but also to play baseball. If there are no adults around, so what? If the boy is enjoying himself, and getting good physical workouts at the same time, that's really what baseball has to offer him.

This, of course, should be a matter of choice. Forcing a boy to play baseball is wrong. I don't care if he's the best player in town. If he doesn't want to play, he's keeping someone who does from having a chance. Playing more will make them better players, but that's really unimportant compared to the fact that it provides wholesome recreation and all the other benefits that baseball has to offer a youngster.

In the course of this chapter, I hope that no one feels that I've been too rough on Little League. Also, I want to point out again that, for the most part, I've used Little League to describe all programs for youngsters of the pre-teen age. (That's the price Little League pays for its success. Now they know how Johnson & Johnson feels when the firm hear all kinds of small bandages referred to as Band-Aids.)

If I've been rough, that wasn't my intention. I've seen first-hand the dedication that goes into these programs. I've seen the work done by a man like Sid Loberfeld, who gives unsparingly of his valuable time, and of his money, to make baseball enjoyment available to a lot of kids he doesn't even know. I've seen the hard work done by league officers, managers, groundkeepers, parents, everyone who volunteers to help the boys. And, most important, I've seen the smiles on the faces of the kids themselves.

But I do want to point out, because I feel it very deeply, that there are cases of abuse in all these programs. However well motivated a person might be, the fact remains that the youngsters are the losers. It makes no difference where the fault lies; the loser is always the boy.

I expect that some Little League managers will feel that I'm guilty of second-guessing them. I also feel that a lot of them watch me manage the Mets, and second-guess me. Well, we're all managers, and every manager knows that second-guessing is part of the job. And—who knows?—maybe we're both right.

MANAGING AND ME

On September 23, 1968, we had an off day in Atlanta. I had a meeting that day with my coaches, Rube Walker, Eddie Yost, and Joe Pignatano. (Our fourth coach, Yogi Berra, was at home with his wife, who had just undergone surgery.) The expansion draft was coming up right after the season, and the purpose of our meeting was to discuss the players on our club that we wanted to protect from that draft, as well as the players on the other clubs that we thought might be, or might not be, protected.

The next day we were scheduled for a night game with the Braves. For a few days prior to that game I had had sharp pains in the chest, along with other discomforts that I had never experienced before in my life. As usual, the coaches and I went out to the park early. About four o'clock, the pains started again. They were dull pains, rather than sharp. About like a toothache, except that they felt like they were going into my chest, and coming out my back. As time came around for us to take batting practice, the pain seemed to get a little worse.

Now it was time for the game. We were in the second inning, and I was really starting to feel bad. I called our trainer, Gus Mauch, and asked him to go into the clubhouse with me. I told Rube Walker that I wasn't feeling well, and for him to take over the club. Then Mauch and I went to the clubhouse.

I explained to him how I was feeling, and he decided to call Dr. Rogers, the Braves' team physician. Dr. Rogers advised me to just lie down, and if I didn't feel better in a little while, he'd take me to the hospital for an examination. Instead of lying on the rubbing table, I stretched out on a big table in the clubhouse itself, so I could listen to the game on the radio.

Still there was no relief, and finally Gus said, "Gil, I think you'd better get dressed, and we'll go over to the hospital and let them take a look at you." I wanted to wait until the game was over, but I realized that I was so uncomfortable, there was no point in hanging around.

We arrived at the hospital; I was examined, and the doctor got rid of the pains for me immediately. No pills, no injections, just one simple sentence did it. He said, "Mr. Hodges, you've had a heart attack." Just that quickly, the pain was gone. I guess I was so shocked, I didn't feel anything else. Maybe it's like the guy who has a terrible toothache, right up until he sits down in the dentist's chair.

Whatever it was, the pain was gone. Then he gave me some medication, and from that day to this, I haven't had any more of those pains.

My reactions for the next few days were normal, I think. I worried about my health, I worried about my wife and four children. Even then, I still found it difficult to believe that something like that could happen to me.

Although it doesn't really have anything to do with managing a ball club, I'd like to tell you something about my wife. The night that I was taken to the hospital, she was at home in Brooklyn with the children. She immediately got on an airplane, and flew to Atlanta. From the next morning on, she was with me constantly. Other than Joan, I was allowed no visitors. Because I was in an Intensive Care Section, she'd just sit by the bed, and our conversations were almost in whispers so that we wouldn't disturb the other people who were around us.

From early morning until late at night, she was with me. In order that she might have company at the hotel, our oldest daughter, Irene, came down to stay with her. Irene was there one day, when she came down with mononucleosis. So there was Joan, hundreds of miles from home, spending the day with a sick husband in the hospital, and the rest of the time with a sick daughter at the hotel.

In the language of baseball, a player who gets the job done even when the going gets rough is described as a guy who "hangs in there." I never saw anybody, on or off a ball field, who "hung in there" any better than my wife. I was very proud of her.

But, getting back to Atlanta, I was given assurances by the doctor who was treating me, Dr. Linton Bishop, that I was going to be all right. My problem was, what did "all right" mean? Would I be able to live a normal, healthy life? And would I be able to manage again?

I am a very fortunate man, in many respects. One of the most important of these is the fact that I like what I'm doing for a living. Also, I'm able to earn a good living doing it. Some men have one without the other. Many men have neither. I have both.

But as much as I like my job—and I can't imagine having one that I would like any better—the job still runs a distant second to my wife and children. Joan and I have a son, Gilly, and three daughters, Irene, Cindy, and Barbara. Nothing in the world is more important to me than my family, which doesn't really make me that much different from most men.

"Boundless joy" may be the phrase to describe the feeling in the Gil Hodges household as the New York Mets' manager and his family accept a well-wisher's phoned congratulations, at home, after Gil was named the Mets' manager. Joining Gil are (left foreground) Mrs. Joan Hodges and (right foreground) Cynthia, twelve; in the background, left to right, are Gilbert, eighteen; Barbara, seven; and Irene, seventeen.

Now, here was my problem: Could I continue to manage without jeopardizing my family? If I could, then that would be great, just what I wanted. If I couldn't, then I'd better start looking around for another way to earn a living. I wasn't looking for odds; I was looking for guarantees.

Finally, Dr. Bishop and I had a long talk about it. The doctor assured me that if I did the things I was supposed to do, followed the ground rules that were laid down, there was no reason why I couldn't be as healthy, or healthier, than I'd been before. Also, I could manage.

During the course of my stay in the hospital in Atlanta, and later, while I was recuperating, first in Florida, and later at home, I got a lot of advice. I am sincerely grateful for it, not because of anything special that I learned but because I knew the spirit in which it was offered. The advice came from people who were very close to me, from some who were only acquaintances, and from some whom I had never met. It came in personal conversations, in letters, and even in the public press. I mean it when I say I'm grateful.

Along that line, I'd like to use this book for a very special thank you. Shortly after I got home from Florida, the mailman started showing up with letters from youngsters. Evidently some local schoolteachers had gotten their classes to write letters to people who were ill, and some of them chose me. Some were one-line notes, others a little more involved, and some youngsters even made up poems. My sincere wish for each of those youngsters is that someday somebody makes them feel as warm and as good as their letters made me feel. There's nothing in this book that I mean more than I mean that.

But getting back to the advice: some of it was directed at how I should behave myself as a manager. The idea was that I should explode more often, let off more steam. Some people told me that if I had done that, I would have been less likely to get sick. I don't believe it.

Gil at home in 1953 with his wife, Joan, and his two children, Irene, two, and Gil, Jr., three.

Gil at home in 1969, discussing the manuscript of this book with his dear friend and lawyer, Sidney S. Loberfeld, who was the first radio announcer at Ebbets Field.

I think that if I kept everything inside me, and didn't tell the players when I was unhappy about something, then maybe they'd be right. But I don't bottle things up inside me. If I have reason to be unhappy with the performance or attitude of a player, I tell him. I try to do it effectively without blowing my top. As long as I'm getting the message across, and I feel that I am, then I'm not bottling things up inside myself.

Now that I've had a heart attack, I intend to take better care of myself. I've talked the matter over with the men I feel are best equipped to give me answers, the doctors, and I'm going to keep on managing. I'm going to do it because I like it, but mostly because they assure me that it's not risky, or, at least, not any riskier than any other job might be for any normal man.

I'm looking forward to it, for several reasons besides those that I've already mentioned. For one thing, I think we're going to have a better ball club. I know exactly what a cliché that is, but I really feel that way. There were mistakes made last year that I don't think will be repeated. I feel that I know my players better now than I did when I joined the Mets, and I think they know me better. That's a combination of things that will make a difference over the course of a year. By knowing them better, I should be able to utilize them better. I know that some of them are capable of some things that others may not be capable of, and knowing that is important to me, and to every other manager, from Little League on up.

Also, managing for the Mets' fans is quite an experience. When you hear ballplayers talk about playing in New York, you hear a lot about the fact that there's more opportunity there for a player to pick up extra money. But there's more to it than that. New Yorkers are great baseball fans, and I'll tell you why. When you make an outstanding play in a New York ball park, it doesn't make any difference which uniform you're wearing. I don't mean that they don't root for their home team, but even the other guys get the cheers for a good play. I remember that I used to really appreciate that when I was managing Washington, and one of my guys would make a good play against the Yankees.

I have much to be grateful for to New York. The people everywhere in the city—even in the Polo Grounds when I was a hated Dodger—have been nicer to me than I had any reason to expect or to hope for.

It wouldn't be fair for me to say that I wasn't happy in Washington, because I was. The people that I worked for and the people in the stands were all very nice to me. But I'm naturally happy to be home. I'm very grateful to the management of the Mets for making it possible, by offering me this job. I'm especially grateful to Mrs. Joan Payson, who owns the club; M. Donald Grant, chairman of the Board; General Manager Johnny Murphy, and his predecessor, Bing Devine.

I've been asked about the danger of managers being carried away emotionally during a ball game, and I've explained my feeling about it happening to me. However, I recognize that some managers do have that problem, and every time I think about it, I think about Charley Dressen.

Charley could get all wrapped up in a ball game, and, as a result, he could get excited. Very excited. I remember only too well a time that Charley really got carried away. I was the batter, and I had a count of two strikes and one ball. The next pitch was high and outside. It wasn't close to being in the strike zone, but the umpire called it "Strike Three." I guess I wasn't paying too much attention, because it never occurred to me that the pitch would be called a strike.

It was so wide that the catcher couldn't reach it. The ball started rolling to the backstop, and I stood in the batter's box, figuring that the count was now two and two. Charley saw me standing there and he started screaming, "Run! Run!" I didn't hear him, and Charley jumped up to holler again, and hit his head on the top of the dugout and went down like he'd been blackjacked. I finally got the message, and managed to beat the play to first. For a few days after that, every time I saw Charley rub the sore spot on his head, I'd manage to stay out of his way.

Now I'm getting ready to go back to work. I'm looking forward to it, and not merely because of the heart attack, although I'd be lying if I didn't say that was part of it. But mostly because I like it. Except for my family, it's my life.

There are responsibilities and disappointments in managing. There are also thrills and accomplishments—and laughs. I think that every manager, whether he's handling a major-league pennant winner or a last-place Little League club, can find all these things in managing, if he gives himself the chance.

One of the most amusing guys I've ever been around was Rocky Bridges. He broke in with the Dodgers when I was playing, and I never knew anyone who didn't like him. He's got a great sense of humor. When he was a kid breaking in, he used to work in the winter as a ditchdigger in his home town of Long Beach, California. Did it for several years after he came to the big leagues, too.

Once, while he was playing for the Detroit Tigers, he found himself in a bad slump. A friend of his asked him how things were going, and Bridges started talking about how tough it was to be in a slump. Finally, the friend said to him. "Well, Rocky, it beats digging ditches, doesn't it?" Rocky stopped, thought about that for a minute, and finally said, "Some days it does, and some days it doesn't."

That sums up any job, I guess. Even managers who win the pennant have some bad days along the way, I suppose. I don't really know, but I'd sure like to find out.